HumanRightsism
True Freedom and Ownership Rights for **ALL** of Us

ALSO INCLUDES

The Handbook for the Awakening Hero

PETER J. WILSON

Thinking Is Free Publications

TACOMA, WASHINGTON

Peter Wilson/Thinking Is Free Publications
photomusicart@yahoo.com

Book Layout ©2013 BookDesignTemplates.com

Ordering Information:
Major Online Book Sellers

HumanRightsism/ Peter J. Wilson. —1st ed.
ISBN-13: 978-1499333329
ISBN-10: 1499333323

Contents

i

Disclosures and Disclaimers

"Lucia Anaya" and "Phil Harper" are fictional characters created by the author and have no association with any real people, living or dead. Any similarities to real people would be purely coincidental.

Dedicated to All Who Seek to Better This Ol' World

If we are not prepared to think for ourselves, and to make the effort to learn how to do this well, we will always be in danger of becoming slaves to the ideas and values of others due to our own ignorance.

—William Hughes, Author of "Critical Thinking: An Introduction to the Basic Skills"

"Forget the politicians. The politicians are put there to give you the idea that you have freedom of choice . . . you don't. You have no choice. You have owners. They own you. They own everything. They own all the important land. They own, and control the corporations. They've long since bought, and paid for the Senate, the Congress, the state houses, the city halls, they got the judges in their back pockets and they own all the big media companies, so they control just about all of the news and information you get to hear. They got you by the balls. They spend billions of dollars every year lobbying . . . lobbying, to get what they want . . . Well, we know what they want. They want more for themselves and less for everybody else, but I'll tell you what they don't want . . . they don't want a population of citizens capable of critical thinking. They don't want well informed, well educated people capable of critical thinking."

—George Carlin, American Comedian and Philosopher

HumanRightsism: Everyone's Basic Human Rights

YOU ARE TUNING INTO "FOR THE LOVE OF HUMANITY". The show is hosted by Phil Harper.

Phil: Thank you all for tuning in tonight. You are watching 'For the Love of Humanity'. I'm your host, Phil Harper. We continue our series this week on political ideologies. For those of you just tuning in, we have already covered Democrat and Republican thought, and we have also explored socialism and religious-based ideologies.

Tonight we are navigating a little-known perspective with our guest, Lucia Anaya. [To Lucia] Lucia, you call yourself a HumanRightsist. You refer to HumanRightsism as the forbidden tenets of a truly free and just society. Are we breaking the law right now discussing these ideas?

Lucia: Whose law? Anyway, I can say this much with certainty: Actively living the ideas of HumanRightsism is strictly forbidden by all national governments. It is generally forbidden to officially advance HumanRightsism in public schools and universities—and the major media for that matter.

Phil: Major media? That clearly presents no obstacle for this broadcast. Well, we are going to discuss it. What I don't get is this. All governments would declare that they are defenders and promoters of human rights—that is their reason for existing. Yet; you claim that truly promoting and defending basic human rights is forbidden by government people.

Lucia: A HumanRightsist upholds two simple and honest statements of basic human rights. I will demonstrate shortly that every member of this audience agrees with these simple honest statements—for themselves and their non-government neighbors.

A true HumanRightsist, however, consistently applies the statements to all humans, including "government" humans and those living in foreign nations. Insuring that "government" humans respect basic human rights is the forbidden element. The basic human rights statements themselves—the most important statements in all human existence past to present—are consciously understood by a minority of truth seekers.

Phil: So, what I believe you are saying is that most folks live day-to-day respecting the basic human rights of their neighbors. A HumanRightsist agrees with such behavior, but also is consciously aware of the two statements that describe our basic human rights. Furthermore, a HumanRightsist recognizes that government humans must also properly respect those same basic rights.

Lucia: Well put, but let's note that "government" humans are actually just a bunch of fellow humans. We hopefully are past the notion that they are gods, or some specially endowed group of wise and virtuous sages. They are just the jocks, the geeks, the divas, the preppies from your and my home room—only now they wield unimaginable power.

Therefore; it is reasonable to consider holding these "government" folks—who are now backed by massive firepower and the threat of prison cages—to the same standard of respectful interaction as the rest of us.

Phil: Lucia, imagine you have the attention now of the entire world. As a HumanRightsist, what would be your brief statement to the world?

Lucia: [Pause] [To audience] For centuries, majorities of populations have allowed for the existence of special little groups of "government" people who need not respect our own and all others' basic human rights. To this day, most of us continue to support these special groups of "government" people. Meanwhile, these "government" people are committing massive levels of murder, fraud, enslavement, and ongoing extortion against millions of peaceful humans at home and abroad.

To move toward a free and just society, we must all come to recognize the following: No matter what services these "special" groups of people claim to provide for us, there is no valid reason to grant them license to violate our basic human rights. I condemn these special groups of criminals, and I condemn those who support them in their criminal activities.

When enough of us have awakened to this truth, we can all peacefully withdraw our support, and effectively prevent further massive violations. We can finally free ourselves to discover new and better ways to respectfully interact with each other and the natural world.

Phil: According to you, our audience members can help alleviate massive suffering for all by becoming HumanRightsists. Why else would someone consider this perspective? What's in it for them?

Lucia: [To audience] First; let me clarify what it won't do for you. It is unlikely to get you a high-level job in "government" or in "government"/business partnerships (also known as corporations). Banking and other financial players will find your ideas to be incompatible with their activities. Those who seek the path of more money and/or power—right and wrong be damned—will find little of interest in HumanRightsism.

On the other hand, to those seeking to live meaningful lives, who seek to take actions that move this world toward greater freedom, justice, and creativity, I offer an amazingly simple and well-reasoned set of principles that do just that. They are based on a consistent and uncompromising respect for basic human rights.

Furthermore; other popular political perspectives require contradictions and specious reasoning to justify their ideas. This just adds confusion for those who seek to promote free and peaceful interaction.

In contrast, HumanRightsism offers clarity that will cut away all that nonsense. Then, you can look at banking and money issues with fresh eyes. The blinders are removed and you see clearly the violators and the victims in the marketplace, the courtrooms, and the fields of battle.

Phil: How did you come upon these ideas?

Lucia: The vast majority of humans worldwide—billions of humans—are suffering from institutional violations and economic fraud. My journey began when I recognized that I share responsibility for all that suffering. Let me tell you it is a life-changing event when that happens on a deep level. I am also responsible for all this violation, so how do I stop contributing to more murder, fraud, and slavery, and become an actor for greater peace and freedom?

Phil: Many will hear that and say you must have a Messiah complex.

Lucia: I would assure them that, for all who awaken to this realization, it is quite the opposite. It was utter humility to understand that I have been so weak and delusional. I have been, and I still am supporting the murder and the very economic injustices that I abhor. The solution does not solely lie with me (and God help us if it ever were to). It lies with a new way of understanding peace and violation, a way that guides one to consistently promote freedom and justice and to defend the innocent from further violation.

Phil: Then perhaps you have a guilt complex.

Lucia: Guilt involves a set of thoughts encountered while focusing on the past. If there are amends to make, make them and move on. Reality is happening here and now. All actions, whether respectful or violational, are, in reality, occurring now. Therefore;

I have confronted guilt and found it to be generally ineffective for my new life as a HumanRightsist.

Responsibility is a different matter. Break that word into two words: response ability. I have the *ability* to *respond* to the situation.

Phil: You are violating people?

Lucia: I am not directly violating people. However; I hold a share of responsibility. When I speak I can encourage peace or violation. When I take hold of another's hand I can do so peacefully or violationally. When I offer support to another, I am empowering either a violator or a respecter of rights.

Everyone I know who is over ten years old pays taxes. Willingly or unwillingly, we all are empowering the activities of "government" people. Many rally for and vote for politicians. Millions suffer daily as those very politicians violate others' basic human rights. If I help to pay an assassin's fee, if I rally for his support in my community, do I not hold a share of responsibility for the murders he commits?

Phil: Many will hear your statements and still refuse to accept any amount of responsibility for the violations you describe.

Lucia: They are also responsible for myriad peaceful interactions occurring daily.

Phil: They may choose to be positive thinkers and focus on that.

Lucia: Wars are happening now. More bombs will destroy innocent people—people who are powerless to defend themselves—as soon as the current rounds have dropped. Right now, "government"-controlled money systems are depleting honest, hardworking folks of their earnings while savvy con artists build ridiculous wealth at their expense. At this very moment, millions of people, who were never proven to have violated anyone, are confined in cages.

Positive thinking and negative thinking are useless substitutes for reality-based thinking.

This is a good time for me to point out that I engage in the peaceful discussion of ideas. I do not seek to manipulate others into agreeing with my point of view. I certainly don't seek to score debate points, so I can high-five those who already agree with me. Such superficial discussions are already abundant in popular media and social circles.

Competitively seeking to "win" arguments has not reduced institutional violence. Honest and respectful discussions will inspire us to stop supporting violational institutions. I promise a fascinating and intelligent journey into forbidden realms of thought and I welcome all aboard.

At the outset of the journey I make this first assertion: You and I hold a share of responsibility for the ongoing violations that "government" people are perpetrating. I advise everyone to question the three A's—*authorities*, their *assumptions* and their *assertions*.

As for me, I am not asserting any special authority. Millions have already come upon the principles under discussion, and, likewise; any audience member would as well if he or she were to inquire deeply into the nature of peace and violation.

I make no claim to special wisdom or saintliness. As my friends and family can assure you, I am generally a fool. Therefore, you will certainly want to question all assumptions and assertions that will follow.

But, if you are seeking to discover deeper truths concerning human suffering, I urge you to accept or reject my assertions by the process of reason. This requires intellectual courage. If you find my assertions to be true, and you remain committed to intellectual integrity, you will likely find yourself accepting ideas that were previously distasteful and quite uncomfortable.

For example, many people are uncomfortable with expanding our freedom. We have all had painful experiences that arose from freely interacting with others. For better and worse, the human mind associated all the elements—good and bad alike—that were involved in the painful experience. Emotionally, the mind seeks to avoid all the elements that were involved. Reason—critical thinking—must be engaged to reclaim the good elements we have abandoned.

As a child, you may have spoken freely and received a harsh and painful response. To protect yourself emotionally, you subsequently chose to abandon speaking so freely. The mind persisted in associating 'speaking freely' with the painful feeling of rejection that resulted.

But now more than ever, speaking freely is the ticket to a better world, as I hope to demonstrate tonight. Questioning popular ideologies can arouse painful responses of rejection from others who are attached to those ideologies. But the rewards are immense as you free yourself from a mental prison of contradictions and incongruities encountered in those popular ideologies. The journey begins here. Your boarding pass requires acceptance of this first assertion.

If you agree, then, you will be curious enough to come aboard and journey a bit further. If you steadfastly hold the conviction that your actions have no effect on the levels of peace and violation among humans, you will find the rest to be pointless.

Phil: Alright then, let's get to the bottom of this forbidden ideology. I gather it concerns human rights. What's the big deal about human rights?

Lucia: A hermit in the mountains who never encounters another human being will have little concern for human rights. For all others—those who interact with fellow humans—human rights are of utmost importance. They set the guidelines for acceptable interactions between people. As we shall see, without basic human rights, all actions a person takes upon you and your family are acceptable and just. No action whatsoever could be identified as violational if no one has basic human rights.

Basic human rights are also necessary to determine what actions may rightly be taken by those who help govern the activities of a community.

A HumanRightsist focuses on only two statements that describe our most basic human rights. I will prove to this audience that all of them already agree with the statements; the statements are indeed the bare-bone essential ingredients of just interaction among humans.

When people interact in accord with the statements, we all enjoy the highest levels of creative expression and productivity.

In a truly free society, some people may choose to live self-sufficiently with little need to earn money, if that is their preference. Or, as most prefer, they may opt to provide services, food and other products, respectfully and freely, so they can successfully exchange for others' services and products.

Trust increases, opening evermore social, business and artistic possibilities.

On the other hand; when people act in opposition to the statements, violation is happening. We all lose trust in each other. We live in a state of fear and emotionally-charged competition, ever watchful for the next abuse of our very bodies, minds and hard-earned properties. We watch what we say and do, confining ourselves to the limited activities permitted by self-declared rule-makers and their hired enforcers. Naturally, our wonderful potential to share our unique gifts with each other is squashed when these basic human rights are constantly violated.

Phil: In essence, when basic human rights are consistently recognized and respected, all people feel secure in their homes. They are free to peacefully and fearlessly pursue their own dreams in their own unique ways. When they are violated...

Lucia: The conditions of life become more and more unacceptable to the extent that violation of those rights is happening.

Phil: Are we establishing criteria for a valid statement of basic human rights?

Lucia: We have a good start. A valid statement of basic human rights must indeed define the parameters of acceptable human interactions. Conversely, the absence of the rights described would make life unacceptable for any rational human being.

By definition, a basic human right must also apply to each and every human.

Phil: That is clearly suggested in the word human. The term does not specify a particular group of humans.

Lucia: Right. Additionally; a basic human right cannot be taken from their possessor, no matter what authority others claim to have. While a person or group of persons may fail to defend their basic human rights, or even choose not to defend them, they can never give them up.

Phil: They are inalienable. That is clearly suggested in the word 'basic'.

Lucia: Yes, because these rights are basic, they are so fundamental to the experience of being human that you or I could not give them away and still maintain an acceptable human experience.

Furthermore; a statement of basic human rights must describe an obligation of rightful conduct that humans can realistically honor while interacting with others.

Phil: I suspect you are referring to the word 'rights'.

Lucia: Yes Phil. As we shall see, a right involves a just claim of ownership. When a person or group of persons holds a just claim to anything, an obligation automatically exists for another or others to honor that very claim.

Now, if it is not possible for another or others to honor the obligation required by a stated right, then the stated right is utopian and pointless, making it invalid for a HumanRightsist.

Phil: Could you provide any examples of valid and invalid human rights statements?

Lucia: Sure; many folks would subscribe to the statement, "people have a right to institutional medical care at others' involuntary expense". The same folks may hold that "people have a right to institutional education at others' involuntary expense". Let's add "people have a right to housing and a daily diet of healthy food at others' involuntary expense".

If all people universally hold such claims, and were to demand fulfillment of the obligation built into those claims, the situation would be untenable.

On the other hand, the following statements are quite easy for others to honor: "All people have a right to freely and respectfully procure education for themselves and others". "All people have the right to freely and respectfully obtain healthy food and medical care for themselves and others". I use the term "respectfully" to denote an interaction that does not violate another's basic human rights. "All people have a right to freely and respectfully procure an adequate shelter for themselves and their families". Let's be sure to add, "All people have the right to freely and respectfully help others as they please".

Phil: I can honor those latter statements by simply not interfering in other people's efforts to better their lives.

The first statements, on the other hand, got me thinking of my travels in India. Every day, I was confronted by hungry and homeless people seeking my help. I threw coins in some cups as I could afford, but, according to your first statements, I was violating hundreds of men, women and children every time I walked the streets and failed to honor all their claims to healthy meals, housing, and medical care at my involuntary expense.

Lucia: No kidding. How far could you have gotten had you tried to honor all such claims?

Phil: On my budget, perhaps a family or two would have been possible at the time. Fulfilling the obligation much further would have put me in their situation.

Lucia: Suppose it were true; they all had a right to healthy food and adequate shelter at your involuntary expense, and many decided to enforce it. Perhaps you would have then exercised your right to healthy food at others' involuntary expense. Why not shelter, education and medical care at others' involuntary expense as well?

Phil: The situation would have become, well, untenable, as you said. I was recently attacked in my own community by three guys. They used a taser and threats to obtain financial help at my involuntary expense. I certainly find such interactions to be unacceptable.

Lucia: Would it have helped any had your neighborhood voted approval for such an action?

Phil: [Laughs] No, that would have been more disturbing.

Lucia: We'll touch on that more in our discussion. I must add that the invalid statements contain another flaw. They contradict valid statements of basic human rights. For example, while in India, the enforcement of your obligation to fulfill the stated right "All people have a right to healthy food at others' involuntary expense" would have required violating your basic human rights. This final qualification is a well-recognized principle of valid reasoning.

Of course we have yet to determine our statements of basic human rights. For now we are just establishing that valid statements of basic human rights cannot be self-contradictory. In other words, they cannot properly prescribe the violation of basic human rights.

Phil: To sum up, valid statements of basic human rights must establish the most essential parameters of acceptable human interactions. Valid statements must be universally applicable to each and every human. They must describe rights that are inalienable and that bestow obligations upon others that are possible for those others to fulfill. Finally, they cannot properly be self-contradictory.

Lucia: Yes, I am asserting that a valid statement of basic human rights must comply with all of those conditions. Remember, we are discussing the most essential guidelines for just interaction between humans. It is crucial that each member of the audience weigh in for themselves on these assertions. The assertions will serve as valid assumptions henceforward.

Phil: To use an old analogy, I sense you are attempting to provide a solid foundation for free and just human interactions, and these assertions must be validated by our audience to verify that our foundation is sound.

Lucia: We certainly desire a sound foundation when it comes to matters of peace and violation among humans.

Phil: Before we get down to building our foundation of basic human rights, I suspect that many of our viewers would question the necessity of doing so. There already exist statements of human rights. We have the Bill of Rights in the United States Constitution. Also, there is the Universal Declaration of Human Rights put out by the folks at the United Nations.

Lucia: Such documents are a political mix of valid and invalid statements of human rights. Let's be independent critical thinkers and come up with statements that meet all the criteria for valid statements of human rights. One can then see how they match up with statements manufactured by would-be rulers.

Phil: Yes, let's get down to business!

Lucia: Okay, let's explore together and come up with our first statement of basic human rights. Keep in mind we want a valid statement that we all agree sets the most essential parameters for acceptable human interactions.

In order to arrive at a statement of basic human rights, let's use a real-life example for the purpose [looks at the camera]—you, the viewer. Since each viewer currently resides in a unique setting, let's generalize a plausible setting for this exploration, a setting you may find yourself in now, or could aspire to in the near future:

You are in your home. Imagine it to be a modest shelter containing only the most essential furnishings and food necessary to maintain a decent quality of life for you and your family. It is situated on a small piece of land that you have acquired ownership of according to the conventions of your community.

In the front yard, you maintain a small garden for fresh herbs, fruits and vegetables. Inside the house, you have some furnishings—a table and chairs, a bed, etc. for comfort. Furthermore; you have gathered food for yourself by trading some of your assets with others.

All these things are justly-acquired property, such that you have a valid claim to ownership of them. This includes your favorite sandwich prepared just so, and placed upon the table before you. Through years of honest work, you have acquired these various properties according to the conventions of your community.

At this time, you are tired and hungry. The children are upstairs—sound asleep—and you would like to relax and eat the sandwich in peace. You pick up your sandwich that you have prepared to your liking—lightly grilled, the havarti cheese melted—when, (HEY), a strange man enters the house, grabs the sandwich from your hands, and takes a huge bite!

He throws the rest against the wall. As you try to object, he pushes you to the floor and wrests the shirt you are wearing off your body. You try to stop him, but he is stronger. Annoyed by your struggles, he ties you up, gags you, gropes your body, and drags you into a closet.

You can hear him talking on the phone—something about finding your money and disposing of your body. When he finishes *with those tasks, he says, he will check the rest of the house for other people to have his way with.*

It looks like you could use a fellow HumanRightsist right about now. Perhaps one of your neighbors is committed to defending basic human rights. It so happens that your neighbor, Kathy, is so inclined. Like all HumanRightsists, she is a critical thinker, although her husband, Karl, is not.

Fortunately, you and Kathy have previously agreed to look after each other and you have given her the keys to your home for the purpose.

Kathy suspects that something is amiss at your home and investigates.

In order to defend you from violation, Kathy needs to be clear on what your basic human rights are. Then; she must discern whether those basic rights are being violated, in which case she may determine to take action to defend you from the violator. By definition, in the realm of human interaction:

Violation occurs when a human or group of humans actively disrespect the basic human rights of another human or group of humans.

And so we return to the question, what are your—and every other human being's—basic human rights?

Your HumanRightsist neighbor, Kathy, and her husband Karl, have observed the stranger climb over the fence that marks the boundary of the property you own. He trampled across your carefully-tended garden, and entered your house. Having been authorized by you to help defend your basic rights, Kathy continued to watch the stranger's activities within your house and is alarmed by what she witnessed. Why?

Kathy is a HumanRightsist, and therefore; she recognizes that:

True ownership rights are your basic human rights.

Her husband, Karl, by the way, is not in agreement with that statement. We'll see how that plays out for you in a moment. As you lay helpless in your closet, fearing for your own and your children's lives, you are likely very clear that your ownership rights have been violated, but just in case, let's explore ownership and how it relates to violation among humans. A good definition of ownership follows:

"Ownership is the socially-supported power to exclusively control and use for one's own purposes, that which is owned." [wordiq.com]

Notice the conditional phrase 'socially-supported power'. While you were alone with your sandwich—with the children secure upstairs—the phrase 'socially supported power' was of little concern to you, for your exclusive control of your home and children, your own body, and your sandwich was uncontested.

However; at this time, a human—who does not respect property rights consistently—has entered the picture. You are in the picture, and now, there is the stranger who has taken action upon the sandwich and upon your body. Also involved are your neighbors, Kathy and husband Karl.

The stranger, in this instance, has actively contested your right to 'exclusively control' the property, the house upon it, its contents, and, quite notably, the children, and the very skin and bones you inhabit. In other words; he has actively contested your claim to ownership of those things. By his words and actions, the stranger has asserted an invalid claim of ownership upon your properties, children, and your body.

Suppose that his claim of ownership concerning the properties in question—and the children, along with the body you inhabit—is a just claim. If that is the case, then no violation can be said to have occurred, even as he proceeds to finally kill your body, and dispose of it, as he plans to do. In this case, no-one, including your neighbor, Kathy, need intervene on your behalf, for there is no violation occurring.

As you lie on the closet floor, feet and hands bound, worried for your children, and awaiting a violent death, you likely disagree with that position, but; minus a rightful claim of ownership of the land property you inhabit—marked by a fenced boundary—along with the house situated upon it, the children and the possessions within—the money and the prepared sandwich—and the very skin and bones you occupy; minus your rightful claim of ownership of all these things, where is the violation? The stranger would have just as much right to control and use for 'his own purposes', the property, the sandwich, money, children and the very body you inhabit.

Let's check in with your neighbors, Kathy and Karl, who at this point are the only other witnesses to the events so far described. This is where the phrase 'socially-supported power' takes on greater significance. Kathy's husband, Karl, believes owner-ship rights are over-rated, that they are something only rich, greedy, selfish people advocate. As far as Karl is concerned, the stranger could be starving and desperate, and therefore entitled to your food, home, and money. Besides, Karl has always been jeal-ous of your friendship with Kathy, and it's none of his business what's going on at your property. Somewhere in his brain, he knows violation is occurring, that, if it happened at his house, he would assert and defend his claim of ownership, but, if he just leaves it alone, this might work out favorably for him.

So much for neighbor Karl. He is not consistent. He will defend ownership rights when it is in his interest—when it con-cerns his claims of ownership. In Karl's defense, the great majority of citizens are not so very different from Karl as they may like to believe.

At this time, two humans are not socially supportive of your 'power to exclusively control and use for your own purposes' the property and the body you inhabit.

Fortunately for you, there are two people who do support your claim of ownership of your justly-acquired properties, the children and your body and mind—you and your neighbor Kathy. Hopefully, Kathy is calling other like-minded neighbors who are willing to take action to defend your rights, and restore peaceful interaction. In other words, hopefully she is seeking to *defend the innocent*.

(If you, the viewer, are thinking 'call the police', that may be a good call. Hopefully, they have a quick response in your neighborhood, and hopefully they are determined to effectively defend the innocent, and not just to apprehend the violator after he exits. There are police officers who are committed to defending basic human rights, and, unfortunately, there are many who are committed to simply enforcing "government" laws and protocols regardless of basic human rights.)

I hope it is becoming clear that without meaningful claims of ownership—of our earnings, our justly-acquired properties, and our very bodies and minds—there cannot be any meaningful human rights.

Phil: The stranger could have easily respected my basic human rights by simply walking on by.

Lucia: Pretty easily! Every violation occurring right now could just as easily be resolved. Every violator could simply stop what they're doing and leave the other person or persons, or their respective properties, alone...violation stops.

Phil: Many object to exclusive ownership of property. "Property is theft" I've heard people say.

Lucia: Those people won't object to having a sign on their home that welcomes all to take any food, money, books and family heirlooms. It could read:

"No-one claims ownership of anything here. Any and all are welcome to enter the bathrooms and the children's rooms anytime and take actions as you please."

If such people claim no right to own those things, there is no violation when others utilize the home and its contents as they may desire. Actually, they needn't even post a sign, because no consent would be called for. We just need to know which peo-

ple don't care for ownership rights—it is a free-for-all at those lo-
cations.

Phil: I can't see that as an acceptable situation for anyone.
Concerning your home invasion scenario, I imagine that every
rational person would allow that violation occurred in every action
the stranger took.

Lucia: And I repeat; minus your rightful ownership of—
your 'right to exclusively control'—your property, the food and
money within, and the very skin and bones you inhabit—there
would be no violation.

As we determine our first statement, a statement that sets
the most basic parameters of acceptable human interaction, imagine that the stranger honestly doesn't know he is violating you in
any way whatsoever.

*Having found your money, he opens the closet door and
un-gags you, enabling you to declare, "Hey, you are violating my
basic human rights."*

*Imagine further that he responds in earnest, "Honestly, I
am not familiar with basic human rights. I've been criticized many
times before that I violate other people's rights, but no-one has
ever taught me what those basic human rights are. If you teach me
what your basic human rights are, in one succinct phrase, so I can
remember it, I promise to respect your and all others' basic human rights."*

Phil: Thank goodness, an opportunity for me to get out of
this mess and to teach this stranger how to interact with other hu-

mans, including my family members, in an acceptable manner. I better get it right.

Lucia: Right, so let's think it out a moment. In your mind, what rights has he violated?

Phil: Well, my right to eat my sandwich in peace without some thug invading my space, stealing my stuff and abusing me and my family physically.

Lucia: Why is all that a violation?

Phil: Because the property, the house, the money, the food, the children, and the body he plans to kill belong to me. I am the rightful owner, and I have not consented to any of his actions.

Lucia: Ah, you have a rightful claim of ownership to those things. You have a rightful claim to exclusive control of those things, and he has not respected your claim so far.

Keeping in mind that the home, money and properties comprise the essential things you need for an acceptable life experience—a dignified existence some would say—in your community, I propose the following statement of Basic Human Rights. For the purposes of our current discussion, we are restricting our statements to those humans who have attained a socially-recognized responsible age:

Every adult human being has the basic human right to full ownership of his or her body, mind, and justly-acquired properties and earnings.

Let's say the stranger seeks clarification.

He asks the following question— "By full ownership, do you mean the power to exclusively control those things?"

You are all too happy to further his understanding— "Yes", you answer.

The stranger inquires further, "And every human I interact with has the right to exclusively control his or her body, mind and properties?"

"Yes", you assure him.

He then wonders aloud, "I've given my word to respect everyone's basic human rights, according to your teaching, but I am anxious as to whether I will be able to attain ownership of the things I require to live well. If I consistently respect others' ownership rights, how may I provide for myself? How do I justly acquire the things I need and desire to live a satisfactory life?"

This seems a reasonable concern to you, so you indulge him further, "There are two basic ways to respectfully acquire ownership of such things. One is to find land, shelter, food and other provisions that are not yet justly claimed by any other human beings and to claim ownership of those things for your-self. If that is not to your taste, you may respectfully negotiate terms with other humans that enable you to respectfully transfer ownership of their properties to yourself."

Phil: That effectively defines 'justly-acquired' property in the first statement of basic human rights.

Lucia: Yes, and you want that to be clear for our apt pupil as he learns how to acquire properties from others in a just and peaceful manner. He is catching on quickly.

"Ah", he says, "I must obtain their voluntary consent!"

"Yes", you answer, "As a respecter of basic human rights, you will always have to obtain another's voluntary consent to take actions upon their bodies or acquire control of their things."

Phil: The stranger has just renounced his heretofore-favored options for obtaining others' properties. At the same time, he obviously has a strong desire to acquire more from others. Perhaps he is hungry and without shelter. What hope has he to acquire these things while also respecting others' rights?

Lucia: Of course, in the stranger's case, he may be greatly disadvantaged by his previous actions. We establish trust with others by consistently respecting their basic human rights. He will need to establish a reputation for respecting others' basic human rights. Once he restores trust, we can offer him the second basic human right which is derived from the first statement:

Every adult human has the basic human right to honestly and respectfully interact with other humans and the natural world free of coercion and the threat of coercion from other humans.

Phil: I see how this statement is derived from the first statement. It follows that, since I have exclusive control of my body, no-one may rightfully take action upon it or threaten to do so...

Lucia: So long as you are interacting respectfully and honestly.

Phil: I see potential trouble with the term 'respectfully'. Various cultures have their own ideas of what comprises respectful interactions.

Lucia: And not just every culture. Every individual has opinions concerning that topic, from appropriate lengths of skirts to the use of vulgar language and how someone shakes hands. Our discussion concerns the violation or respect of basic human rights. Therefore; for HumanRightsists, the answer already exists in the primary statement of basic human rights.

A respectful interaction is one in which all humans involved are respecting each other's ownership rights. Again, you must acquire others' voluntary consent to acquire their property or take any actions upon their properties or persons. That can translate just fine for all cultures and languages, from the wilderness tribes of Brazil and New Guinea to the highly controlled peoples of the United States, Sweden and North Korea.

Having established that most basic definition of respectful interaction, you or I can rightfully assert our own personal definitions of respectful interaction. I can choose to not do business with those wearing mini-skirts, who use obscene language, or have weak handshakes. Of course, I eliminate opportunities to do business the more I qualify my own definition.

Phil: Others will surely snatch up those business opportunities.

Lucia: In a free and just society, you can be certain of that.

Let's say that I am foolish and primitive enough to refuse to do business with people of darker skin tones than myself. I am not violating anyone's rights in doing so, because I have full ownership of the shop and its contents, as well as my own mind and physical form. In my community, word will spread quickly, and I will likely suffer dramatic reductions in business.

Others, who are free to offer the same goods and services and who are not so restrictive in their customer base, will acquire my lost opportunities for sales. Not only would those other shops acquire all the customers who have darker skin tones, but they will further gain all the customers of lighter skin tones who reject my ignorant views.

Actively asserting racism and bigotry in such a manner is bad for business. Those who refute such attitudes will be rewarded with the esteem of the community and higher sales.

Phil: So the two statements of basic human rights do not eliminate racist attitudes and other forms of bigotry?

Lucia: There are no celebrations for racists and bigots at the HumanRightsists' table. We promote consistent respect for each and every person's basic human rights according to the two statements.

However; valid statements of basic human rights define violations that may rightly be defended by force if necessary. Racist and bigoted attitudes exist among nearly all cultures and ethnic backgrounds.

Attempting to enforce the prohibition of such attitudes would introduce a whole new level of violent and fear-ridden interaction among people. In Central Africa, so-called Hutus have attempted to resolve the bigotry of so-called Tutsis with violent force. Tutsis have done likewise, and violence escalated accordingly.

Today, many voices there call for respecting all members' basic human rights, and, to the extent that Hutus and Tutsis have heeded the call, violations have subsided dramatically.

An activist HumanRightsist defends any and all people whose basic human rights are being violated—regardless of ethnicity, religion, sexual orientation, or level of wealth. A HumanRightsist consistently promotes the right of any and all people to respectfully interact with others and the natural world free of coercion and the threat of coercion.

Utopian goals, in this case, eliminating racist thinking and bigotry, cannot be achieved by forceful action. Such actions would also contradict both statements we are establishing to set the parameters of just and free interactions among humans. A HumanRightsist supports the use of necessary force to defend innocent people from racist actions, only insofar as those actions violate another's basic human rights. A HumanRightsist cannot rightfully take the forceful action necessary to eliminate racist thoughts or beliefs. The challenge of eliminating racist thoughts and beliefs, a worthy challenge indeed, must be met peacefully, without violating basic human rights.

Phil: A community of HumanRightsists, then, is not a utopia.

Lucia: You will still find people who have prejudices, people who are selfish, some who don't want to share with others, some who choose to avoid this or that person, and others who aren't very loving or kind. Forcing people to interact without prejudices, to be selfless, to share what they own, to fraternize equally with all, to act lovingly or kindly, is un-achievable and would clearly involve violating their rights to full ownership of their bodies, minds and justly-acquired properties.

On the other hand, all members of that community will be able to honestly and respectfully interact with other humans and the natural world free of coercion and the threat of coercion from other humans. Their homes and other properties and earnings will be secure for their use. They won't be molested, raped, killed, kidnapped or unjustly caged by others.

They will therefore be free to offer services and goods in trade with others so that they may further enrich their own lives and the lives of others as they are capable and willing to do so. Those who are kind, sharing, loving and open-minded will certainly be rewarded with richer opportunities as others are attracted to such qualities.

Respecting basic human rights according to our two statements is immediately achievable for any given human who commits to do so. Likewise; all rational people would find it essential that other humans respect their basic human rights when they interact.

Phil: Yes, I should think every rational person in any culture would object to someone taking actions upon his or her body, earnings and properties without his or her consent.

Lucia: And every rational person does object to such violations, unless he or she is either threatened with additional violation, or is the victim of a con job.

Phil: Can it really be so simple, that the parameters of acceptable human interaction are defined by two statements?

Lucia: I am asserting as much. As always, I challenge you and the audience to explore the validity of that assertion for yourselves. Every courtroom case involving a claim that a person or group of persons violated another person or group of persons is predicated on the basic human rights as described by the two statements. This includes cases of alleged trespass, theft, fraud, assault, battery, kidnapping, enslavement, extortion, murder, mass murder, and genocide. All allege that somebody took ownership control of another's or others' bodies and/or properties without obtaining the consent of those rightful owners.

Phil: You stated earlier that the statements of basic human rights were "the most important statements in all human existence past to present". I clearly see what you mean.

If we reject the statements, we are at a loss to determine any violations occurring among humans. If we allow the statements to be valid, all the actions taken by the stranger in the home invasion were violational—from the moment he trespassed my property line, including, thank goodness, the part where he groped my body and tied me up! And I unreservedly condemn all the actions you just listed, from trespassing to genocide, which clearly violate people's basic human rights.

I don't directly engage in such actions, and I venture to say most of our audience members do not directly engage in such actions.

Let's say that all of us are on board with you—that humans are best served respecting each others' basic human rights in accord with the two statements. We must respect others' rights to full ownership of their own bodies, minds and justly-acquired properties. Furthermore; we allow that all others have the right to respectfully and honestly interact with others and the natural world free of coercion. Are we HumanRightsists? Mission accomplished?

Lucia: I'll start with the good news. For most of us, throughout the world, the answer is a qualified "Yes". We generally agree that human interaction must properly abide the two statements of basic human rights.

I interact with hundreds, perhaps thousands of people, day after day. I exchange goods and services, drink beers with others, go on dates, enjoy creative diversions and I interact with the natural world. Throughout, I encounter only rare occasions of violation among my fellow "private" humans.

Likewise; I've traveled to many countries, including those of Europe, Asia, North and South America, and I cannot recall a single incident of violation in all my interactions with private members of those countries. As a HumanRightsist, I celebrate every day the general recognition of and respect for basic human rights.

Phil: I detect the crucial qualifier when you refer to "private" humans.

Lucia: "Private" is the word we are offered to designate humans who do not identify themselves as "government" people.

Phil: I suspect we are entering the forbidden zone at this point.

Lucia: Were I to restrict my discussion to private humans, my ideas would be welcome in nearly all circles. Depending on my level of creativity, effective self-promotion, and fortunate timing, I may propel myself to the highest ranks of celebrity as achieved by Mother Teresa, Martin Luther King, and the Dalai Lama.

Phil: That may work out well for you, but it will be a letdown for our audience. We're here to bite into the forbidden fruit.

Lucia: Then I will seal my fate, once again, to remain in relative obscurity. Ironically, the most important discussion of all time has also been the most unwelcome in popular circles. That is changing.

At the beginning of our discussion, I stated that billions of people are suffering the effects of institutional violence and economic fraud. I promised that a commitment to the statements of basic human rights offers clarity that cuts through the contradictions, deceits and confusion that plague political ideologies today.

Most importantly, I stated that once you are fully aware of these rights, you will see clearly which people are the violators and who are the victims in the marketplace, the courtrooms and the arenas of violent conflict.

Phil: Between humans, I can now determine that the violators are those who violate others' basic human rights.

Lucia: We are watchful, then, of burglars, muggers, those who would assault us, etcetera, and we universally condemn their activities.

Phil: Such people are clearly violating basic human rights according to the statements.

Lucia: And I said earlier that every human objects to violations of their basic human rights unless...

Phil: Unless threatened with even worse violation or they are victims of a con job.

Lucia: In all modern societies, we have groups of humans who claim special authority to violate the basic human rights of all the other folks. Sadly, most of those other folks have, willingly and unwillingly, submitted to the perpetual violation of their basic human rights.

Phil: What an atrocious set-back if that's true. We just accomplished the task of determining our most basic human rights, and come to find that most humans have surrendered them to a minority group of humans. And this is the case throughout the world? Who are these humans who claim special authority to violate the rest?

Lucia: While the particulars vary, they are generally a group of people who declare special membership in organizations they call "The Government".

These "government" people clearly violate the basic human rights that we've determined with our two statements. They confiscate honest people's money and properties—without obtaining the consent of the owners—on a massive scale; they commit acts of extortion; they abduct and imprison folks who have not violated anyone; they control honest people's business activities through intimidation and threats to bring them to ruin; they maintain and violently control a fraudulent money system that makes them and their select partners very rich and powerful at the expense of honest and productive people; they pay thugs to intimidate and murder people in other countries.

Phil: But we've agreed that the two statements describe the parameters of acceptable interactions among humans, and that those parameters are immediately achievable for all humans who commit to abide them. It makes no sense that any community would allow for such exceptions. How is it that most people worldwide have surrendered their most basic human rights to these groups of humans within their communities?

Lucia: As stated earlier, rational people will only surrender to violation if they are either threatened with worse violation, or they are unwitting victims of con artists. In most countries, both threats and con games attain the necessary submission of the masses.

We can easily identify cases involving threats of worse violation: "Give me your money or I will assault you", "Give up your money or I will confiscate your home", "Submit to being locked in a cage or I will club you and possibly shoot you".

On the other hand, identifying the fraudulent activities of con artists requires more rigorous critical thinking. It is absolutely essential that our audience engage their critical thinking skills.

Phil: You've insisted as much throughout our discussion. Why the added emphasis at this point?

Lucia: When a decision involves high stakes, we must engage our skills of critical thinking. The higher the price, or greater the risks involved, the more we must question the three A's mentioned earlier.

Phil: Authorities, Assumptions and Assertions.

Lucia: Yes. We question, and we are not satisfied until we are presented with valid reasons and evidence. Then we question again.

Imagine yourself a passenger in the back seat of a car, parked on a private driveway. The driver of the car is a virtual stranger to you, and he plans to back the car into the public roadway behind you. Let's say that public roadway is a quiet neighborhood street with a posted speed limit of 20 mph.

How rigorously will you engage critical thinking skills as the driver starts the engine and puts the car into reverse? The risk of serious harm to you is low. You may note that the driver is apparently sober, fasten your seatbelt, and hope for the best. In other words, you may require very little in the way of valid reasons and evidence to justify the actions underway, even as the driver commits to entering the public roadway. You may not even bother to look up from your smart-phone to acquire evidence that the driver is choosing a good time to back safely into the street.

Now; re-imagine the scene, changing only one factor. Instead of a quiet neighborhood street, the driver is now planning to back the car into a busy highway with a posted speed of 70 mph. The risk and potential cost of the planned action is high, so that critical thinking must rise to the occasion accordingly.

You will not be so easily satisfied with the driver's credentials. You now question your assumptions about the driver, the vehicle, and the planned course of action. Are the reasons for choosing to back into traffic valid? Is there a safer way? Instead of checking e-mails on your smart-phone, you will likely be watching the traffic, acquiring evidence that the maneuver is being executed safely.

Phil: I get your point that higher risk and cost calls for higher levels of critical thinking. You claim that the vast majority of humans have abandoned their basic human rights to a smaller group of humans in their respective homelands. You've pointed out that the risks and costs are extremely high. Are you suggesting that these billions of people have simply failed to engage in critical thinking?

Lucia: For most, that describes the situation.

Phil: In that case; as with backing a car into high-speed traffic, it would be wise indeed for every person to engage their critical thinking skills when it comes to such grand scales of violation.

Lucia: Without critical thinking skills, we cannot effectively promote and defend our own and others' basic human rights. We can't possibly reverse the massive violations occurring daily, unless we all engage our critical thinking skills as the high stakes demand.

Phil: Well let's see this critical thinking in action.

Lucia: Okay, let's engage critical thinking. First, let's familiarize ourselves with the stuff we'll be chipping away at.

We know we will be questioning "government" people's claims to *authority*, along with their *assertions* and *assumptions*. We know that we mustn't be persuaded to any degree without valid reasons and evidence. Our critical thinking tool is becoming sharp. Let's sharpen it further.

In place of valid reasons and evidence, con artists provide fraudulent justifications to advance their proposed actions. As we shall see, they cannot justify their intentional acts of violation with valid reasons and evidence. After all, we are seeking a world of increasing peace, justice and freedom, and intentional violation on a massive scale doesn't resonate with that goal. According to our statements of basic human rights, it is clearly the opposite direction to what we are seeking. So they substitute made-up reasons, outright lies, and insubstantial evidence in order to "justify" what are clearly violational actions.

I'll refer to the use of fraudulent justification as 'rationalizing', a common term among advocates of critical thinking. A HumanRightsist requires valid reasons and verifiable evidence when evaluating actions and proposed actions.

Phil: Critical thinking again.

Lucia: Billions must require valid reasons and evidence, if we are to reverse the epidemic of violational institutions worldwide. In doing so, people will see through the rationalizations and awaken to the calling that millions of HumanRightsists have already answered—the call to consistently defend the innocent and to promote free and peaceful interaction among ALL people.

Phil: "Government" people control school systems that program hungry young minds how to think...

Lucia: And especially what to think, which is limited to viewpoints they deem to be acceptable.

Phil: They also have partnered with all the major providers of TV programming, movies, magazines, and newspapers to further reinforce this limited range of thinking. How can our audience members arm themselves with the thinking skills needed to unravel such a barrage of propaganda?

Lucia: They must discover for themselves the most important thinking tools. These are tools that government folks, their schools, and their media partners refuse to address—sound principles of free and just interaction among humans.

Phil: Such as: 'Every adult human being has the basic human right to full ownership of his or her body, mind, and justly-acquired properties.' Also: 'Every adult human has the right to honestly and respectfully interact with other humans and the natural world free of coercion and the threat of coercion from other humans.'

Lucia: You've been taking excellent notes. We've spent a good deal of time establishing those two principles and now recognize them as our statements of basic human rights.

We've also noted that the vast majority of humans, with the exception of government humans, abide them as they interact with each other. This has been an amazing achievement in the last couple centuries. Historically, three major groups of humans have generally been excluded from these statements of human rights.

Phil: Slaves.

Lucia: Yes, having a clearly-designated enslaved class of humans absolutely contradicted our statements of basic human rights.

Phil: Women.

Lucia: That's a very large group of humans. Fully recognizing basic human rights for women and human-beings that were designated as slaves used to be forbidden topics.

While there have been some major advances for these two groups, the third group has barely registered on the radar—non-"government" people. I refer to all humans who are not identified as "government" people or their "corporation" partners. This includes all skin tones, cultural identities, sexual orientations, genders, those of low and high income, gay and straight, the employed and unemployed, people of all religious persuasions from atheist to Christian, Buddhist, Hindu, Jewish, Taoist, Muslim, Wiccan, all people—foreign and local—and the young and old. Fortunately, this is changing.

We can endure another thousand years of "government-decreed" violation of us all as we fight each other over special-interest labels. The tide will turn dramatically when a critical mass of us awaken from this dream of special-interest identities, and recognize the simple truth: Each and every one of us is a human being, and therefore has the very same right to full ownership of his or her body, mind, and justly-acquired properties. Each and every one of us has the right to honestly, respectfully, and freely interact with others and the natural world.

Phil: That seems so much simpler and honest. Why do media folks remain so preoccupied with divisive issues: racial divisions, religious differences, ethnic conflict, political party battles, vilifying foreign peoples, the rich versus the poor?

Lucia: As with all other con artists, "government" people must distract their victims. They must prevent us from questioning the actual violations they are perpetrating against ourselves and foreign people.

With our statements of basic human rights, combined with critical thinking skills, we can ignore the fictional divisions of humanity, and focus clearly on the violators themselves.

Phil: Violation is happening when a person or group of persons violate others' basic human rights.

Lucia: Exactly, so here then is the con game in play: While it is unacceptable for "non-government" people to violate others' basic human rights, it is magically acceptable and supposedly necessary for "government" people to violate everyone else's basic human rights.

Phil: That is odd, to say the least, since, as I said at the beginning of our show, most "government" people and their advocates assert that we need special "government" people in order to defend and promote our basic human rights. Why do most people accept such a blatant contradiction?

Lucia: Of course, there are as many reasons as there are individual humans. Many simply believe they make personal gains from "government" people violating basic human rights. Whether such actions are violational or not is inconsequential for them. Many have simply not thought it through. Most people, however, do care whether they are supporting acts of thievery, fraud, extortion, kidnapping and mass murder. Such people, and I believe there are billions, are the focus of my work.

Phil: So; good caring people approve of an institution that commits ongoing violations against billions of non-"government" people—people who are not violating anyone.

Lucia: These good, caring people fear that the alternative would be worse. They have been taught by well-meaning—and not so well-meaning—teachers, law enforcers, corporate "news" writers and trusted news anchors, talk shows, "government"-funded scholars and professors, and often their own friends, families and neighbors—just a wide range of "respectable" and smart folks—who assure them that eliminating the violational practices of "government" folks will lead to horrendous consequences.

Phil: So many "authorities" have taught us that, so it must be true!? And since truly defending everyone's basic human rights would disrupt their preferred status quo, the above-listed "authorities" aren't going to give much airtime to our two statements of basic human rights.

Lucia: So it is. All of us must take the initiative to question these "authorities". "Government"-associated teachers, law enforcers, corporate news people, scholars and professors all make gains and maintain their comfortable lifestyles so long as things stay the way they are. A consistent respect of everyone's basic human rights would require major changes. Therefore; promoting HumanRightsism is out of the question, as far as they are concerned. Do such people likely have a bias that favors the existing "government" system? That's a good question to ask your-selves daily? Can we simply trust such people to inform us, on any meaningful level, of current "government" actions that are violating our ownership rights, and our rights to freely and respectfully interact with others?

Phil: I would require valid evidence and reasons to back up their assumptions and assertions.

Lucia: No wonder you have your own show. You have already jumped a major hurdle. Most of us have been trained since earliest childhood to not question authority. We were allowed, maybe even encouraged to question where rain comes from, why the ocean appears to be blue, and how a forest of massive oak trees can grow from a hand-full of seeds. But when it came to rules that restrained our freedom to interact with others and the natural world, such questioning was not to be tolerated.

Questions like "Why can't I go out and play?" were met with the answer we all received at some time—"because I said so". Never mind why. If we received additional "reasons", they involved some bogeyman to inspire fear.

And so began the end of meaningful inquiry concerning "authorities" in our lives. Some of our complaints may have been tolerated so long as we complied with the rules.

When we got older and freed ourselves from the restraints of our parents, we confronted a powerful group of rule-makers who used similar methods.

Only now; chores gave way to laboring for "society" in the form of taxation and the persistent burden of monetary inflation; timeouts and groundings became jail sentences and further losses of rights; spankings were up-leveled to bullets and bombs.

Never mind that these rule-makers had been our peers growing up—just fellow kids—playing kickball on the playground, and raising their hands when they knew the answer in the classroom.

Phil: Now, those kids have ultimate control of my home, my earnings and my activities. You'd think we all would want to seriously question such a state of affairs.

Lucia: My sentiments as well. As I already mentioned, we have been trained to refrain from such questioning, but we all are capable of reversing our habitual submission to these authoritarians.

Therefore; I urge all to break free of the mental chains that have been reinforced by self-proclaimed authority figures since early childhood. You all are grown up now, and are quite capable of thinking for yourselves. I can persuade, I can urge, I can insist, but I have neither the power nor the right to make that happen.

Phil: I can't speak for our audience members, but I'm on board. I do question the authority of these rule-makers, especially when they claim exemption from the obligation to respect our basic human rights. Now that I am willing to question the authorities, their assertions and assumptions; what's next?

Lucia: We must properly begin with questioning the very legitimacy of so-called "government authority". We have all been taught since childhood to respect and honor the authority of our parents, and, as a matter of course, the "government" systems—particularly the "government" folks—operating in our respective communities. Before we explore the legitimacy of current claims of such authority, let's spend a moment on ancient con artists and their specious claims to "government authority".

Nearly all of us can see through the superstitions that deluded earlier communities of people into submission. That will provide some momentum as we trek into modern rationales used by today's rulers.

Ancient rulers claimed divinity to justify their license to control and abuse the others. Even through the Middle Ages, kings claimed some divine right to own the population of folks within a particular region. Popes and Bishops have also claimed to be authorized by the big guy upstairs.

People eventually awakened from these absurd delusions, necessitating a more sophisticated con game. People recognized that a dignified existence requires true ownership of their own bodies and properties.

In place of God, self-declared rulers have created lofty documents to justify their ownership of people and land masses. One such document is the Constitution of the United States of America.

Many of the drafters of this famous document were well aware of our true basic human rights (for white propertied men anyway).

However; the final draft not only failed to meaningfully acknowledge basic human rights, it further claimed special license for a few hundred egomaniacs with control issues (politely referred to as The Congress and the Executive) to violate millions of folks nationwide.

Today, such violation occurs on a massive and ongoing scale. One key provision in the U.S. Constitution states "The Congress shall have Power To lay and collect Taxes, Duties, Imposts and Excises, to pay the Debts and provide for the common Defence and general Welfare of the United States...".

Phil: Taxes, duties, imposts and...what?

Lucia: Excises.

Phil: I didn't realize they had synonym dictionaries back then.

Lucia: It must have been quite a brainstorming exercise to come up with four euphemisms for taking a person's property without their consent. Suppose they had used accurate words— "The Congress shall have the power to steal, rob, loot and plunder the properties and moneys of the general populace as Congress may decree...".

Phil: That absolutely defies our statements of basic human rights. It might as well grant the so-called Congress and Executive the power to kill innocent people.

Lucia: That one is covered as well: [The Congress shall have Power...] "To declare War, grant Letters of Marque and Reprisal, and make Rules concerning Captures on Land and Water"...

Phil: It doesn't explicitly state that members of Congress have the rightful power to kill people.

Lucia: Describe a recent war that did not involve intentionally killing innocent people. Anyhow, yes, we find more euphemisms.

'Declaring war' sounds official and vague compared to 'Congress shall have the power to license invasions of other people's lands, confiscation and destruction of their properties, along with large-scale murder and kidnapping of the people who make their homes in those lands.'

Further, granting letters of marque and reprisal is a euphemism for 'Congress shall grant people license to commit acts of piracy.'

Phil: It is absurd to empower a few hundred people to license such wholesale violations. How would a true HumanRightsist have worded that section of the Constitution?

Lucia: Respect for basic human rights allows for defending people from violation, so that the following provision would have been valid and just: 'Congress shall call for and organize volunteer forces to defend communities from invasion and other evident violations of basic human rights.'

Of course a document that legitimately promotes and defends basic human rights would clearly state our basic human rights—"It is hereby recognized that all people have the following basic human rights: The right to full ownership of their bodies, minds, and justly-acquired properties and earnings, and, the right to honestly and respectfully interact with other people and the natural world free of coercion or the threat of coercion by others.'

The fact is the U.S. Constitution was not written for the promotion and defense of basic human rights. That was and still is the sales pitch. It certainly is not a valid contract, since a valid contract must involve the consent of all parties involved.

It is a document that bestowed ownership control of a large mass of land and it's populace to the very group of men who wrote the document, and little more.

Another key provision depriving the general populace of basic human rights follows: The Congress shall have the power "To coin Money, regulate the Value thereof, and of foreign Coin, and fix the Standard of Weights and Measures".

Phil: How does their coining and regulating money violate my basic human rights?

Lucia: If you and I could freely accept and utilize their money or opt to use other forms of money as we see fit, there would be no violation. That is not the case. "Government" folks require that we conduct business in their currency. Business people must collect and pay numerous taxes in the form of "government"-approved currency, or the business owner will be threatened with devastating fines, jail time, and the loss of their business.

That wouldn't be so bad if the "government"-approved currency was a sound one and retained its value. The opposite is true. "Government"-approved money is fraudulently-produced and anyone would be foolish to save it for future needs, because it will lose its value quickly. You don't need a PhD in economics to recognize that ain't good money.

Phil: Speaking of economics, I've always assumed the subject of money creation and banking are too complex for most of us, and so it's best to leave it to the experts.

Lucia: Phil, you are right concerning the "government"-approved production and distribution of money. It is so corrupt and irrational that the top experts can't make sense of it. Complex textbooks and college courses attempt to justify the "government"-controlled system. Many people want to get very rich without providing valuable goods and services to others. Thanks to the fraudulent money system, such people can tap into the corruption that abounds in the realms of politics and financial deal-making.

On the other hand; a sound money system, based on the consistent respect of our basic human rights, is quite simple, as I promised earlier, and requires no special study at all. Here it is:

As HumanRightsists, you and I—and every other human being—may freely and respectfully determine how and with what we conduct exchanges.

Many would likely choose gold and silver as mediums for exchanges. Others may prefer bartering, work credits, or vouchers tied to certain valuable businesses. All such moneys would be in keeping with our second statement of basic human rights: 'Every adult human has the right to honestly and respectfully interact with other humans and the natural world free of coercion and the threat of coercion from other humans.'

Phil: I grant you that that was a very short course in economics, but can it be practical in the real world of commerce? Won't it be chaos if we all are free to use whatever currencies or barter methods we choose?

Lucia: Let's agree on a definition of 'chaos'. Webster's offers the following definition that is apt for our discussion: Chaos is "The inherent unpredictability in the behavior of a complex natural system...".

Human interaction is inherently unpredictable, so that my answer to your question is yes; billions of people freely choosing which currencies and other methods of exchange best suit their respective needs will result in unpredictable behaviors and outcomes.

People who want monopolistic government-enforced currency will predict horrible behaviors and outcomes for such a proposal. And on the other hand, those favoring a truly free approach to money will likely predict a thriving, secure, and creative community. By virtue of respecting basic human rights, it would inarguably be a just approach to trade.

Due to the chaotic nature of human interaction, we are unable to verify with certainty either prediction. A person would have to be endowed with precognition. A critical thinker does not abandon basic human rights to those claiming omniscience or precognition.

Remember that my purpose here is to find agreement with our audience as to what truly constitutes our basic human rights— the essential parameters of acceptable and just interactions among humans. As we discussed, nearly all humans agree with the two statements of basic human rights arrived at earlier.

On the other hand, documents like the U.S. Constitution declare that a minority of people shall be excluded from abiding the parameters of those basic human rights—and not because they are the most just and wise among us; not because they have consistently proven themselves to be honest, compassionate, and charitable; and certainly not because they are sworn to consistently promote and defend our most basic right to ownership of our respective bodies, minds and justly-acquired properties and earnings. Not at all.

The document grants a small minority of people power to violate the many only on condition that they follow the procedures outlined within the document itself.

Their decision to enforce their own preferred monetary system gave the minority of ruling people immense power and control. Tragically, it has disempowered the vast majority of productive people—the rest of us. It facilitates the confiscation of our earnings by way of "taxation", a euphemism for extortion when perpetrated by "government" people. Further, it provides for the most devious method of theft ever devised—intentional devaluation of the "government"-enforced currency, also known as planned inflation.

Phil: But the U.S. Constitution grants that citizens may vote for—and therefore choose—those who are to hold such powers.

Lucia: For a HumanRightsist, having some token role in choosing which humans shall violate the rest of us is no comfort. A majority of people deciding on a given course of action does not of itself make that action wise or just. A gang rape, a lynching, a large army invasion of innocent villagers; none of these would be justified by first taking a vote among all those involved.

On the other hand, accordance with well-reasoned principles—such as our statements of basic human rights—is the sound approach to determining just and peaceful actions.

Phil: I'm on board with the statements of basic human rights. However; we've all been taught that there are special situations wherein even the most basic human rights must be disregarded.

Lucia: Are you open to questioning those assertions and the authorities who make them?

Phil: Well, I'm not comfortable knowing that a group of people claim ownership control of my body, my property, and my honest earnings, based on a document that I never agreed to.

Yes, I think, in light of the ongoing violence and fraud being perpetrated by "government" people, the time has arrived for all to question this group's special license to disrespect basic human rights.

Lucia: You are now open to the most exciting explorations into peace and violation among humans. Let's wait a moment for our audience members to catch up with you. There is little point in their continuing the journey if they aren't ready to question the assertions and assumptions they've been taught. [Pause][Some laughter from the audience can be heard]

Phil: We'll just have to assume that those choosing to stay with us are ready to explore.

Lucia: Excellent. As I will demonstrate, we are dealing with con artists who have sophisticated tools to bury truth, so it will be necessary for us to obtain some powerful tools to dig up and expose the truth. As I stated earlier, our tools are principles we may add to our statements of basic human rights.

Phil: How do principles help us to unravel the propaganda of con artists?

Lucia: Principles are accepted valid assertions by which we can judge present or proposed actions. Do the actions under consideration align with or contradict the accepted principles?

We have already established our first two principles—they comprise the two statements of basic human rights. These two statements are enough to invalidate and condemn the systemic violational actions of "government" people.

Unfortunately, these con artists have convinced most people that "government" people are necessarily exempt from respecting others' basic human rights.

To dig up the true nature of these con artists' assertions, we must add additional principles. These four principles will help anyone who confronts the rationalizations of would-be violators. I call them the four rationalization-busters.

Phil: Catchy. I think we all confront rationalization often, perhaps daily.

Lucia: These rationalization-busters can be handy for challenging personal rationalizations, like having a cigarette when you've committed to quitting, but they truly are essential as we choose to support or directly take part in actions concerning thievery, extortion and murder among humans. Here is the first:

'No human can know with certainty the true motives residing in another's mind.'

A given human can post their goodly intentions in the New York Times, have it announced by famous news broadcasters, and get the Pope to declare them to be truthful, and we will still be unable to know with certainty the true motives of that individual.

Phil: In politics, people who violate other people tend to have the purest intentions, don't they?

Lucia: Yeah, according to them. I almost forgot to mention—because it seems so obvious—that con artists tell lies.

"Government" con artists are no different. With their lies, they create an illusion for the uncritical thinkers who blindly trust authorities in "government", media, and education positions. In this way, they succeed in arousing fear-based confusion.

The result is delusion among lazy dependent thinkers. Yes, sophisticated con artists present elaborate and convincing lies to gain the cooperation of others. If lying about their motives can effectively gain your cooperation, and, given that we are unable to read their minds, we can reasonably expect a con artist to resort to stating false motives. It is the first step to gain support for their proposed violational actions.

Phil: Goodly intentions are a typical rationalization for violational actions, especially when they are offered by "government" people.

Lucia: Yes, con artists apply gobs of pretty makeup and perfumes to their violational actions so that the nasty actions appear desirable, or at least tolerable. But this only works on lazy dependent thinkers.

Sound principles strip away the makeup and perfumes, enabling critical thinkers to see the ugly pus and warts—that were there all along—and to fully smell the rotten stench of violation that others are senselessly putting up with, perhaps even celebrating.

Phil: I think we can see this in action if we choose an example. How about drafting young men into military service? That always struck me to be an obvious violation of basic human rights.

Lucia: Well, if I did it to you, the actions would accurately be labeled as kidnapping and enslavement. Also, I would be guilty of reckless endangerment of your life, along with several counts of inducing you to commit acts of destruction of property and murder. Wow, would I be in trouble.

And you would certainly be in the right if you were to take forceful actions to defend yourself from such grotesque violations. Perhaps, even deadly force would be called for in order to defend your basic human rights.

Phil: I think we can all agree you would be perpetrating horrendous crimes against me. However; when "government" people do the same to fellow humans, millions are convinced there are no violations occurring at all. Are such people just plain stupid?

Lucia: Not necessarily. They may be quite brilliant in their respective fields, but they are not thinking critically on the issue at hand.

When "government" people institutionalize such acts of kidnapping, forced labor, slavery, and inducement to commit criminal acts, they are sure to meet resistance from those being violated. As with all con artists, these "government" people will not disclose the true nature of their violational actions.

They create new terms, so that kidnapping, enslavement, inducement to commit murder, and invasion become words like "drafting", "conscription", "deployment", and "Operation Just Cause". This is simply a process of burying the truth. For example, the term "conscription" comes from Latin and literally translates as "to write down together"—you know—like you and me, co-writing an essay or a play. That is a far distance from you and I 'terrorizing and killing strangers in foreign lands together'.

Unfortunately, changing the words is enough to satisfy millions that the motives are pure, and that violation is no longer occurring. Learned professors, the New York Times, and trusted news broadcasters all repeat the same specious terminology, so names such as "Operation Just Cause" officially take the place of accurate terms. In this case, 'invasion', 'bombing' and 'violent takeover' would have been accurate descriptions of the U.S. Attack on Panama.

Phil: But we're critical thinkers and we are defenders and promoters of basic human rights.

Lucia: Glad to hear it Phil. Of course, "government" people coercing young men—who are not violating anyone—into slavery conditions and compelling them to commit criminal acts against others is a blatant violation of those young people's basic human rights according to our two statements.

Phil: We already established that our statements of basic human rights describe the bare-bones parameters for acceptable human interaction. I would not find it acceptable to be kidnapped, enslaved, and compelled to violate other humans' bodies and properties—not to any degree whatsoever. How do these perpetrators convince others that such violational actions are acceptable?

Lucia: As I've said, they cannot do so with valid evidence and reasons. They must invent stories that involve unverifiable motives. Therefore; we recall the first rationalization-buster—"We cannot know with absolute certainty the true motives residing in another human's mind". Of course, the violators will state the noblest motives to justify horrible violations. Since we are unable to reliably read their minds, we must demand valid reasons and evidence to back up their stated motives.

As we have often observed, they typically avoid that problem altogether by claiming the need for secrecy. Beyond presenting pretty and noble motives, they will further make supernatural proclamations. They implicitly claim powers of omniscience and precognition. They will tell stories in which they amazingly are able to read other people's minds. They will claim the ability to accurately predict outcomes of complex human interactions—all for the purpose of arousing fear.

When people are confronting a real and present danger, no-one needs to coerce or con those people to take action. Most people will rally to defend themselves and loved ones. When there is no real and present danger, "government" people often rally support by arousing fear.

Phil: I can't think clearly when I'm in a state of fear.

Lucia: When fear is aroused, critical thinking is the first casualty. Just as airline pilots have rational protocols for emergency situations, we must have a set of sound principles to handle challenges concerning human interaction.

Phil: "Government" people tell us that—as much as they may violate innocent people's basic human rights—the outcome of their actions will be a desirable one. Likewise, we are taught that "government" people must take violational actions, such as initiating more taxation or additional wars, or awful things will happen to us all.

Lucia: And yet; isn't it an awful thing to initiate war? We may challenge such assertions with our second rationalization-buster:

In the realm of human interaction, no human can know with certainty what will be the long-term outcome of a proposed action—violational or non-violational—initiated upon a population of people.

When discussing small groups, large groups, or millions of humans, each having unique characteristics, ambitions, concerns and activities—the long-term outcome of any given action cannot be determined with certainty.

It's a bit like throwing a feather into a tornado and determining where it will end up tomorrow. There simply are too many variables. This is true in the realm of human interaction as well.

I can't even determine how my mate will react to an action I take with any serious degree of accuracy, much less my entire community of unique humans—humans responding to unsurmisable sets of variables—each carrying unique past experiences, cultural backgrounds, fears, and desires. What about an entire nation of humans?

I can make an educated guess; I can speculate, postulate, but; no matter how much information I gather, I'm still venturing a guess—the product of my imagination at best. I may have PhD's, be a respected authority, an expert. I may be looked upon as a very wise man. I'm still applying my imagination—along with my biases, wishful thinking, and knowledge deficiencies—to produce my own best guess concerning the future outcome of a chosen action upon the realm of humanity.

Phil: I follow that, according to the first rationalization-buster, we can't know another's motives with certainty. Now, with the second one, I see that, even if a "government" person's motives were pure and honestly communicated to us (which could happen), we would still be unable to know the future outcome of his or her proposed actions.

Lucia: And further; what if the "government" person's proposal involves violating people's basic human rights? We are not conned by their stated goodly motives, thanks to Rationaliza-tion-Buster One.

Now, we are not to be conned by their claim to know the future. According to our Rationalization-Buster two, the goodly outcome that he or she assures us will result from the violational action is not possible to predict with accuracy.

Phil: I think I'm getting it. When "authority" types, in-cluding "government" officials, professors, and corporate media folks, engage in fearful speculations, they consistently propose "solutions" that involve violating thousands or often millions of peaceful humans.

Lucia: If those actions are violating innocent people; that is, if innocent people are being coerced into giving up their money and their properties; if they are being abducted, caged and/or murdered, any notion of just action has already been lost.

There are additional principles—sound and irrefutable—that clarify the muddied waters served to us by these con artists.

This brings us to our third rationalization-buster:

For every challenge met by a community of humans; just as there are myriad violational solutions that may be considered, there are also myriad non-violational solutions that may be considered as well.

Phil: One would have to be open to considering non-violational options of course.

Lucia: Today, the term "government" may generally be seen as describing an institution licensed to violate basic human rights, so that the myriad possible non-violational actions are dismissed as a matter of course.

Really, the very thing that differentiates "government" people from the rest of us is this notion that they may properly violate others to get things done.

The rest of us choose from the unlimited assortment of non-violational means to get things done. We negotiate peacefully with others. When we seek another's services, money, or property, we obtain their consent.

If our first approach doesn't meet our challenge effectively, we get creative and come up with additional peaceful approaches. If we run into a really big challenge, we market heavily, we rally for support, or we team up with others.

Yeah, we work to resolve problems. We might have to work harder sometimes. We may have to be more creative.

Fortunately, when compelled to meet a challenge, we find there exists myriad possible means—violational and non-violational—and, unlike "government" people, we ignore the violational ones.

"Government" folks, practically by definition, are those who take the opposite approach. They exclude the myriad non-violational approaches, thereby choosing to obtain what they want through extortion, theft, kidnapping, threatening to confine peaceful people in cages, massive destruction of properties and large-scale murder.

Phil: What a sad state of affairs. According to "government" people, along with their media and academic supporters, the solutions to the world's problems require that peaceful people, who are not the problem, must be violated. But aren't violators the problem to begin with? So, they propose to solve violation by intentionally initiating more violation?

Lucia: that leads us to our fourth rationalization-buster:

In the realm of human interaction; while the intended outcome of a proposed action is the product of one's mind—and, therefore, is unreal—an action taken in the here and now— whether violational or non-violational— IS REAL.

A proposed action, once taken, exists in reality. An action that is actually happening is—how else can I put it—actually happening. If it is a peaceful action, then a peaceful action is really occurring in the world. No guesswork; no speculation. Peaceful interaction is happening and humanity is better off for it.

If a violational action is under way, then basic human rights are being violated in the here and now reality. Greater violation is happening in the world, and humanity is worse off for it. In reality!

Of course, I have given much consideration to these four principles that I call rationalization-busters, so that, for me, they are sound and irrefutably valid. I am not superstitious enough to believe that "government" folks, the people of academia, and those of corporate media, have powers of omniscience and precognition.

However; for you, Phil, and our audience members, these are assertions. That is all they are, until you apply your tools of critical thinking to each of them. Question them mercilessly, and determine their truthfulness for yourselves.

These Rationalization-Busters invalidate all assertions that justify violating anyone's basic human rights.

The simple truth is this: Promoters of violation offer rationalizations rather than reasons. Promoters of peaceful interaction reject rationalizations and demand reasons, simply because every human being has the basic human rights to, one, completely own their own bodies, minds, and justly-acquired property and earnings, and, two, to freely and respectfully interact with others and the natural world.

Phil: Let's say we have used critical thinking—we have truly thought all this out for ourselves—and we all agree that the principles are sound and valid.

The two statements of basic human rights do indeed describe the essential parameters of acceptable interactions among humans, and the four rationalization-busters invalidate proposed solutions that violate basic human rights.

The reality is this: Apart from "government" humans, there are humans who do violate other humans. There are private people who steal from others, who defraud innocent people, who harm others physically, and who rape and even murder others. If we exclude violational solutions, can we resolve such problems?

Lucia: Given that basic human rights describe the most essential parameters of human interaction, a HumanRightsist cannot abide the intentional violation of anyone's basic human rights.

Let's then eliminate all solutions that involve violating people who are not violating anyone, and see what solutions we may find remaining. I encourage all to play this out in your own minds. In your community, you have several people who prefer to violate others' basic human rights. How may we act to correct the situation?

Phil: Stop the violators!

Lucia: Well, there's a novel approach. Now, recall the third rationalization-buster: 'Just as there are myriad violational "solutions" (such as those favored by "government" people), there also are myriad non-violational "solutions" to consider. Let's start with burglaries in your neighborhood.

We are HumanRightsists, so violating innocent humans to restore respectful interaction is irrational and, therefore, is not an option. What can be done to reduce such violation, while increasing free and respectful interaction?

Phil: I understand that having a dog can help. I can make my home more secure with better locks.

Lucia: There are alarm systems. I can arm myself with a shotgun or other defensive weapons.

Phil: Organizing neighborhood watch groups has transformed many neighborhoods. I've seen it first-hand. Perhaps, several neighbors could pool their funds and hire a reputable security service. We could teach children the basic human rights statements, and how abiding them benefits themselves and others in their community.

Lucia: We can go on and on, because there are, in fact, myriad approaches—all non-violational—that we may consider. Any and all may act on the proposals without increasing violation of others' basic human rights. You and I could enact five hundred such proposals, and find that we have not violated a single person's basic human rights. We can apply the same procedure to every challenge currently handled by "government" people today. Many fine thinkers have done so and their ideas are freely available on the Internet, in books, and other media. All stated challenges, from drug abuse to maintaining road systems—even the challenges of reducing poverty and countering foreign invading armies—all may be met with myriad non-violational actions. If a person or group of persons find themselves being violated by others, they will likely seek to take defensive actions. Defending oneself or others from violation reduces violation and restores free and respectful interaction.

"Government" people and their corporate media and education partners consistently propose violational approaches to address challenges. They can only supply rationalizations to support their proposals, but these cannot survive the four Rationalization-Busters. Their approaches, in reality, increase violation and decrease free and respectful interaction, and both are clearly the wrong direction.

Phil: I'd like to give our audience a chance to ask questions with our remaining time. Let's start with this young lady.

Young lady: I get that property must properly be acquired without violating another's basic human rights. Stealing and extortion are not just means to acquire property. Given that, I think many of us still have concerns about how much property a person may acquire in his or her community.

Lucia: I promise to address those concerns, but first let's assess the reality of ownership for the great majority of honest, hard-working folks today.

According to the definition of ownership we are using, ownership is the 'socially-supported power to exclusively control that which is owned.'

At this time, people of humble earnings ultimately own nothing. "Government" people claim the right to control what amount of earnings an individual may keep for their own needs.

Whether a humble person rents or is said to "own" his or her home, that person truly does not have exclusive control of that home. "Government" people claim ultimate control of that property.

What's more, "government" people claim ownership control of people's very bodies, as they forcefully restrict what substances a person may use, what activities they may respectfully engage in—including how they may conduct their non-violational businesses.

If I don't have the socially-supported power to exclusively control my earnings, my property, my own body, I have little to no power to influence the larger course of events in our realm of humanity.

For example, during the latter years of the Vietnam War, the great majority of Americans favored ending the violations going on, but they ultimately owned nothing, including their earnings and their own bodies. Therefore; "government" people persisted in using others' hard-earned moneys and bodies for several more years. The result was more deaths of U.S. Soldiers as well as more death and property destruction in that poor country, despite the wishes of most Americans.

A meaningful democracy requires respect for every single person's right to true ownership of his or her body, mind and justly-acquired properties. Only then does that person have the power to give or withhold support for a proposed action.

Throughout this entire discussion, I have proposed that we all must first recognize our most essential and basic human rights. Each person who does so may then effectively take action to defend and promote those basic human rights for themselves and others.

Only then will honest and productive folks have the power to support—or withhold support—for anything whatsoever.

To answer your concerns about how much a person may own, we first must imagine a community of true owners—owners of their own bodies, earnings and other justly-acquired properties.

In such a community, all members would be empowered to socially support—or withhold support for—others' power to exclusively control that which they own. They could do so without violating anyone's basic human rights.

According to our Rationalization-Busters, there are myriad non-violational actions people may take to meet such a challenge.

Let's try it out: You are living in a community of HumanRightsists, all members truly owning their respective bodies, and justly-acquired properties—including, of course, their earnings. In your community, there is only one grocer, and he is attaining large amounts of money and property. The majority of the population does not want to support his acquisition of wealth any longer.

However; being HumanRightsists, they refuse to violate honest folks, including the now-wealthy grocer. What can be done?

Phil: They could set up a co-op grocery, wherein all may have an ownership share.

Lucia: That could be quite effective, and there are myriad additional actions people could take without violating anyone's basic human rights.

Our wealthy grocer's share of the food market will diminish accordingly, and others in the community will increase their power to acquire foods according to their own preferences. How about a farmer's market? Or maybe people would open small neighborhood groceries. We can go on and on with solutions that don't involve confiscating honest people's money or other properties.

Many fine writers have written extensively on how we may meet challenges of violence, disease, road maintenance, and poverty without violating anyone's human rights. If wealth disparity is your cause, wealth disparities may be adjusted without violating anyone's basic human rights.

In our HumanRightsist community, Phil, you may like the wealthy grocer and may choose to continue supporting his business. On the other hand, the young lady, who has asked the question, and the majority of the community do not care to support his large share of the grocery market any longer.

As true owners of themselves and their money and property, they are empowered to reduce his share of business and to support new suppliers. Returning to reality, the great majority of people truly own nothing. That means that most Americans are not socially-empowered to exclusively control their own selves and their assets. For such people, democracy can only be an illusion.

Phil: An elaborate con.

Lucia: Everyday, more awaken to that.

Phil: We have another question. The gentleman...

Gentleman: I can't imagine a world without some kind of government to assure that justice prevails. I also think it is important to insure that there is a safety net for those in dire need. Are HumanRightsists anti-government?

Lucia: First, I fully agree with your initial statements. I can't imagine a world without some kind of government to assure that justice prevails, and, yes; providing a safety net for those in dire need is a worthy venture.

However; I absolutely oppose, and I will oppose to my dying day, leaving the governing of such crucial matters to extortionists, thieves, liars, con artists, slave-masters and murderers. That accurately describes the top men and women who claim "government" authority in my part of the world.

To   answer   your   question—you   asked,   "Are HumanRightsists anti-government?"—I will need you to be more specific. As a HumanRightsist, I engage in critical thinking concerning important matters of human interaction.   Relationships wherein certain people govern other people are often worthwhile and sometimes necessary for the well-being of those involved. As a HumanRightsist, however; I insist that those relationships include an abiding respect for the basic human rights of all those involved.

While I have been asked, "Are you anti-government" many times, no-one asks the truly pertinent question, "Are you opposed to government that violates basic human rights?"

Gentleman: But that would be an absurd question. No one in their right mind would favor government that violates basic human rights.

Lucia: When that is the case, my current work will be done, and I will focus on other pursuits.

Phil: One of the student visitors from our local university is eager to ask a question.

Student: As a HumanRightsist, do you favor capitalism or are you an anti-capitalist? Are you for a free-market economy or against it?

Lucia: Such terminology has provided distraction and massive levels of confusion and violence, hasn't it?

Do you plan to accept or reject all my assertions based on my answer? For a HumanRightsist, those emotion-laden terms are irrelevant. An interaction between humans is just when the people involved respect each others' basic human rights. It is of small concern whether you label the interaction capitalist, free market, communist, socialist, Marxist, Buddhist, Taoist, Muslim, Christian…blah blah blah.

I can elaborate further if you'd be willing to answer a question for me. What is your preference concerning capitalistic interaction?

Student: I am an anti-capitalist.

Lucia: Please describe the sort of community you would like to be involved in. How would you like the members of your community to interact with each other?

Student: I believe all goods and services should be collectively owned.

Lucia: Would each member have the freedom to consent to or dissent from those terms free of coercion or the threat of coercion?

Student: I haven't thought about that. I guess I'd like to think so.

Lucia: If so, such a model would not violate anyone's basic human rights. It may not be my cup of tea, but, then again, it would be no business of mine, so long as everyone's basic human rights are respected. To address the question concerning whether a HumanRightsist is 'for or against a free-market economy', I would like to know your description of a non-free-market economy. If a truly free-market economy is one in which people have the right to freely and respectfully interact with each other, then, of course, that would suit any HumanRightsist. An economy characterized by institutionally-organized people violating other people's basic human rights—no matter what you may choose to call it—would certainly not be supported by a HumanRightsist.

I hope I'm making it clear that, in and of themselves, labels and specifically-preferred processes are not compelling to a HumanRightsist. Respect for all people's basic human rights is the ultimate blueprint for a truly free and just society.

Phil: Let's take one more question...the woman with the red outfit...

Woman with red outfit: You've explained why you oppose taxation. I follow how it violates basic human rights. But then, how else could we ensure that everyone pays their share in society?

Lucia: What is *my* share? What shall *your* share be? Who should receive my share, and what should they be doing with it? In a just democracy, one with full respect for basic human rights, who should decide these matters? In our current system, a few hundred politicians, hundreds of miles from my home, determine the answers and I am to comply or suffer the consequences.

Let us say that you and I are required to pay taxes that we can't afford right now. My roof has a leak, and you just lost your job and need all your funds to pay rent and buy groceries for now.

Further, let's say the money that the "government" people are demanding from us is to be used to invade a foreign country and gain control of its peoples and resources.

If you and I object to the amount of money and the planned use for it, how may we effectively resolve the situation? Write letters? Protest in the streets? Wait for the next election and hope for the best? You are granted one vote out of millions. Maybe a more just politician will be elected. Some democracy!

Let's examine how much power you and I have in our current situation. Our will is this: we don't want to pay—say, one thousand dollars, and further; whatever amount we may consent to pay, we don't want a penny of our money supporting the invasion that is planned.

According to the current group of "government" people, I am allowed to "petition" the "government" people. Of course, the "government" people have already decided on their taxation and invasion plans. They plan to get the money from you and me, even if force is necessary, so our petitions are not compelling. The letters may easily be ignored.

We can take them to "court", but the judges are all "government" people, who also receive their generous pay and benefits from the very funds we are disputing.

Ah, but we get to vote the next round. We lose this time around—you go hungry, and I abide a leaky roof—but, between us, we have two votes to cast four years from now. In a national election, that will amount to two votes out of millions.

If we are very influential, we can campaign for our favored "representative". Say he wins. No matter what he promised us, he is under no contract with you or me to fulfill the wonderful promises.

Is this far-fetched? Has such a thing never happened? Is he even really my representative? Why is he doing things that I would never agree to?

Furthermore; what about the minority of voters—as many as 49 percent of the voting public—who chose the other candidate as their "representative"? They are simply unrepresented for the next four years? How is that a government of the people?

Only con artistry can twist and contort what is, in truth, government rule by decree—what we and the rest of the world are now living with—and conjure up the absurd notion that we are in a democracy, a government that operates only with our consent.

In the real world, your decision to give or withhold consent would properly reside with you, and likewise, mine with me. Taxation makes our choice to give or withhold our consent a foregone conclusion; our money is taken with or without our consent. Once taken, we have no power to control who receives it and for what purpose it will be used.

Of course, "government" people favor that approach. For thousands of years, various "government" people have been very successful at forcing people to pay their so-called "share". I grant you that. What is virtuous in that fact? Such "government" people have ordered the building of temples, palaces, monuments, yes, and dams, bridges, and roads. They have also initiated war after war—massive events of murder and destruction.

The trade-off has been the disempowerment of the majority of honest and productive people worldwide.

Only a large-scale awakening to the primacy of our basic human rights can lead to our true empowerment...empowerment to defend the innocent from violation and to honestly promote free and respectful interaction—to move toward a better world.

If your interest is to force all to pay a share of their income as dictated by a small group of folks in suits, you already have your wish. If you honestly share my desire to empower us all—including the humblest among us—then you will have to confront the question at hand today, which is this: What sort of society can effectively empower each and every member?

I have asked myself that question, and, year after year, I have returned to my thesis, that a society of people who consciously and consistently defend and promote basic human rights is the only way to empower all members. Ownership of a person's own body, mind and justly-acquired properties—including his or her earnings—is the power for that person to exclusively control his or her body, mind and money.

Would you characterize a woman who ultimately has no power to exclusively control her own choice of activities, a woman who cannot freely choose the fate of her own earnings, a woman who cannot exclusively control her own home, including the flesh and bones in which she resides...would you honestly characterize that woman as an empowered human being? Is a slave empowered?

On the other hand, a prevailing recognition and respect for her right to exclusively control her own body, mind, and justly-acquired earnings and property does empower her—in a real way.

We can further empower her by respecting her right to freely and respectfully interact with others and the natural world. Then, she may freely and respectfully pursue her dreams; she may help others according to her wishes; she may deny support to those she disagrees with; she may associate with those who provide fulfillment, and avoid those who she finds to be distasteful.

As a HumanRightsist, I support such empowerment. The various forms of "governments" we are abiding today do not. The largest propaganda is that taxation and the coercive control of peaceful folks' activities are the only means possible for providing security and essential services to a community. And, yes, we all have been exposed to only that model of human interaction.

Furthermore; that coercive model is the only one permitted by "government" people at this time. Therefore; no-one is permitted to explore alternative approaches, such as one wherein all people, including "government" people, must respect all others' basic human rights.

Without the possibility of such explorations, we are condemned to submit to the demands of violational "government" people.

And so, here we are today, generally acting as bystanders, witnessing the increasing powers of "government" people, abiding their demands for more of our earnings, complying with their fraudulent money system, funding their murderous ventures overseas, and paying for more guns, bombs, and tanks that are distributed to violational regimes throughout the world.

I urge all honest people throughout the world to join the millions of HumanRightsists who are truly defending the innocent and consistently promoting free and respectful interaction for all humans. I call such people Awakening Heroes.

Phil: And that brings us to "The Handbook for the Awakening Hero", a copy of which we are making available to every member of our audience. Would you like to say some words about this handbook?

Lucia: My final words tonight must begin with the most important question: What distinguishes a slave from a free man or woman? Quite simply, the ownership of a slave's body, mind, and properties is claimed by another or others.

If we socially support the slave's ownership rights—including ownership of his or her body, mind, and properties—the term slave no longer applies. Slavery conditions are unacceptable to a HumanRightsist. Having an institution of humans stealing from other humans is unacceptable. Institutionalizing humans kidnapping and locking up humans who are violating no-one is unacceptable. Institutionalizing humans killing humans who are violating no-one is unacceptable. It matters not whether the killers are wearing a fine costume with badges and ID's or they are attired in clown suits.

The two statements of basic human rights, when respected, eliminate all conditions of slavery, theft, kidnapping, and the caging and/or killing of people who are not violating others. Notably, it is easy for all humans to respect each others' basic human rights as prescribed in the two statements.

No rationalization that "justifies" the enslavement of people who are violating no-one can hold up to the four Rationalization-Busters.

Long ago, a group of men claimed control of a large land mass and those taking up residence on it. They wrote up a document detailing how they would maintain control of that land and the inhabitants of that land. The document was approved by other men who likewise claimed an ownership share of the massive acquisition.

None of that can "justify" anyone violating our basic human rights today.

The first step is to simply acknowledge what our basic human rights actually are.

Many choose to denounce ownership rights altogether. Understandably, they want to refute the ruling elite and their wealthy partners' unjust claims of ownership, but a blanket dismissal of ownership rights disempowers us all.

The Awakening Hero engages critical thinking, thereby avoiding such a fatal error. Then, the way becomes clear—true ownership control of our own affairs, our own properties, and our own earnings is our empowerment.

The handbook is for those who are awakening to the true hero's journey: To consistently defend the innocent from violators, and to consistently promote free and respectful interaction—for all humans.

If you choose such a course, you may not have numerous vacation homes, yachts, stocks and bank accounts to bequeath to family in your final moments, but then; what would that accomplish in the end?—Various family members waiting to divide up your accumulated assets? Some of those family members may respect your wile and aggressiveness; perhaps, some will scoff at your luck and cunning as they fight for a share? Who knows?

Join the true heroes so that, one day, wealthy or not, you can honestly say to the children about you, "I did my damnedest to leave you with a freer and more peaceful world—a better world."

Phil: Well, I'm keeping a copy of the handbook, as I test these principles for myself. I may be joining the ranks of the Awakening Heroes. That's all the time we have tonight. Thanks to you all for tuning in to "For the Love of Humanity". Thanks also to our guest, Lucia Anaya, for her insights on HumanRightsism and its currently forbidden tenets of a free and just society. For the love of humanity, this is Phil Harper. Good night to you all, and here's to better days ahead.

BOOK [2]

Guide for the Awakening Hero

THIS IS A HANDBOOK FOR ALL who seek to better this world. As such, you may well fall into one or more of the following callings:

*Permaculture Advocates/ CSA's/ Organic Producers

*Minority Activists

*Activists for the low-income and marginalized

*Corporation Protesters

*Counter-culturists

*Religionists/ Spiritualists/ Metaphysicians

*Peace Officers/ Soldiers Defending the Innocent

*Honorable Politicians

*Health Professionals

*Personal Empowerment Advocates

*Artists Advocating Peace and Love

*Educators

*Scientists

*Philosophers

*Conservatives

*Liberals

*Right-wing, Left-wing, Democrats, Republicans

*All people who seek to move toward a world of ever-increasing justice, freedom and peace for ALL humans

This includes billions of people, so—with so many on board—why does violation continue to exist on such a grand scale? The answer is that the great majority of us believe we are too insignificant and unqualified to better the world, and, therefore; it's not our job to act in this regard. This runs counter to the solution proposed herein, that:

Each and every one of us can and eventually must empower and qualify ourselves to consistently take actions that move humanity toward greater justice, freedom, and consistently peaceful interaction.

My contention is this: If the billions of humans listed above, all sharing the objective of making a better world, could arrive at a set of clear and consistently-applied principles concerning matters of peace and violation, the ideological squabbling would give way to massive increases in peaceful interaction. The defense of innocent and peaceful people would prevail. Yes, I propose living a hero's life, but it is an ordinary hero I refer to. No superpowers are called for—just a few skills—especially critical thinking—and a consistent adherence to defending the innocent and promoting free and respectful interaction.

For those who have read the discussion on 'HumanRightsism' between Lucia and Phil, much of this will be familiar. The epilogue suggests further territory to explore with your critical thinking tools.

The handbook will first define the qualities of the Awakening Hero. Next, we'll explore each quality, starting with critical thinking, as an essential tool for discerning matters of violation. We will utilize that essential tool to define basic human rights, because one cannot determine a violation of another human without understanding basic human rights.

The majority of people I talk to are inconsistent in their determination of human rights and the violation thereof. This is a desirable state of affairs for those who prefer to gain by violating others. Massive levels of confusion among hardworking and productive folks serve to obscure violators' corrupt designs. *Critical thinking* is the cure for confusion and we will then apply it to the two primary objectives of all Awakening Heroes:

Consistently Defend the Innocent from Violators

Consistently Promote Free and Peaceful Interaction

Finally, I will propose four irrefutable principles of free and respectful interaction that defeat any and all arguments advocating violational solutions to the challenges we all face. These are the four "Rationalization-Busters". Oddly, people who identify with modern versions of "government"—institutions that purportedly exist to protect basic human rights—are generally the people who advocate vociferously for solutions that violate basic human rights. Coming in second place are advocates of violation who do not identify with "government"—robbers, muggers, home invaders, rapists, kidnappers, small-time extortionists and con artists.

How to Approach this Book

The "Awakening Hero's Handbook" is not meant to be read through just to simply be accepted or discarded; I invite you to read each chapter progressively, allowing time after each chapter, to thoughtfully verify or reject the ideas presented before jumping into the next.

All of our minds have been cluttered with conflicting viewpoints. You must inquire deeply and honestly to discover the core of peace and violation amongst humans. That's what the Awakening Heroes are doing. If you're up to the task, I welcome you to the most important discussion today.

There are three important realms of peace and violation to confront:

1) A human's conflicts arising within his or her self
2) Humans interacting with the natural world
3) Humans interacting with other humans.

This book confronts the realm of *humans interacting with humans*. Understanding this realm will go a long way to resolving the other two realms. However; all three realms must be explored to move to a better world. Undeniably, they are interlinked, so that improvement in one realm brings improvement to the others.

Disclosures and Disclaimers

I am not an official member of any political, scientific, religious, educational, or corporate institutions, parties or organized movements, including; Republican, Democrat, Libertarian, Communist, Socialist, Anarchist, Christian, Muslim, Judaic, Conservative, Liberal, Tea Party, or any group of individuals seeking to institutionally alter public policy to favor their respective agendas. Any views presented and inferences made herein that are shared by such institutions are coincidental. I concede that I am a flawed human and am as challenged as anyone I know in my personal evolution. While ad hominem attacks and accusations of hypocrisy can indicate the challenging nature of consistently *defending the innocent* and *promoting free and respectful interaction*, they will hardly invalidate the worthiness of the task.

MY THANKS

Thanks to my Mom and my Dad—my personal Heroes—and an immense thank you to my beautiful wife, Stephanie, who keeps on not leaving me no matter how obsessed I get with this stuff, and a big "Thank you" to each and every friend and family member who has acted as a sounding board until exhaustion set in, and "Thanks" to the millions of Awakening Heroes who are already taking actions that are making the world a better place!

The Basic Principles

Violation occurs when a human or group of humans actively disrespects the basic human rights of another human or group of humans.

True ownership rights are your Basic Human Rights.

The Statements of Basic Human Rights

Every adult human has the basic human right to full ownership of his or her body, mind, and justly-acquired properties and earnings.

Every adult human has the right to honestly and respectfully interact with other humans and the natural world free of coercion and the threat of coercion from other humans.

The Four Rationalization-Busters

1) No human can know with certainty the true motives residing in another's mind.

2) For every challenge met by a community of humans; just as there are myriad violational solutions that may be considered, there are also myriad non-violational solutions that may be considered as well.

3) In the realm of human interaction, no human can know with certainty what will be the long-term outcome of a proposed action—violational or non-violational—initiated upon a population of people.

4) In the realm of human interaction; while the intended outcome of a proposed action can only be the product of one's mind—and, therefore, is unreal—an action taken in the here and now—whether it be violational or non-violational—is real.

The Awakening Hero:

Consistently defends the innocent from violation

Consistently promotes free and respectful interaction

Chapter 1

Who Are the Awakening Heroes?

There is a choice we may all stumble upon in the course of our lives—either to continue to live in delusion, consciously or unconsciously contributing to the violent and corrupt existence we all share (the default choice), or, to truly live the hero's journey—a life that is honorable and meaningful, thereby contributing to our evolution into a realm of greater love, peace and creative freedom. This book is for those who, having weighed in, have opted for the heroic life.

Our minds give way to delusion quite easily. We readily believe in our night-time dreams, even when they are inhabited by 8 foot bugs, or humans flying un-assisted. Each morning we awaken to reject such fantastic delusions and we can do the same for our delusions within our "waking" experience. This requires vigilance and a determined search for truth. This requires heroic efforts. In this book, I make the case that individuals like you and me, awakening to such a calling, are the only way this world will move toward one of diminishing violation and increasingly respectful interaction.

I am stating loud and clear that leaving such matters up to institutions—their "experts" and "authorities"—has been the

wrong call for the past 10 thousand years, and will continue to result in disastrous outcomes in the near future. There are already
millions of Awakening Heroes worldwide, and we could use millions more to take action here and now as a check on the violent
policies of modern "governments" and to promote peaceful alter-
natives to the current challenges we face. Let's get started. First,
let's define what an Awakening Hero does.

An Awakening Hero Consistently
Defends the Innocent from Violation

An excellent example is found in the actions of Hugh
Thompson, Jr. during the Vietnam War. While other U.S. soldiers
were following orders and shooting unarmed women and children,
Hugh Thompson, Jr. intervened, defending a group of villagers
from further violation.

Much later, in a hearing on the My Lai events, Chief
Prosecutor, William Eckhardt, had this to say about Hugh Thompson's actions that day, "[Thompson] put his guns on Americans,
said he would shoot them if they shot another Vietnamese, had his
people wade in the ditch in gore to their knees, to their hips, took
out children, took them to the hospital...flew back [to headquar-
ters], standing in front of people, tears rolling down his cheeks,
pounding on the table saying, 'Notice, Notice, Notice'...then had
the courage to testify time after time after time."

We can only now imagine our hero's life following the
massacre and subsequent hearings—the hatred from un-heroic fel-

low soldiers and American "citizens", the death threats, and proposals by control-obsessed congressmen to put him away for treason. What was he up to taking on such a role?

A true hero defends the innocent from violation. I doubt Hugh Thompson Jr. set out to be a hero that day at the My Lai village. He was committed to doing his duty according to his understanding of it at the time. All the same, we can determine that he understood that, while his duty involved providing support for his fellow U.S. soldiers, beyond all else, his duty was to defend the innocent, be they Vietnamese or Americans. Throughout millennia, a hero defends the innocent.

But that isn't a complete description of Awakening Heroes.

The Awakening Hero
Consistently Promotes Free and Respectful Interaction

CONSISTENTLY. Not only when it's convenient. Not just for those times it works favorably for him or her-self, or suits personal causes. We have enough inconsistent "heroes" to fill stadiums. Obscene violations are promoted and committed amidst all the inconsistencies. Most every politician "promotes peace" while initiating wars, economic abuses on innocent people, along with invasions of privacy and the jailing of non-violent humans by the millions. The Awakening Hero will have none of that.

The Awakening Hero consistently Defends the Innocent and consistently Promotes Free and Respectful Interaction.

It sounds simple, but there are many powerful, influential institutions—"governments" and "government"/business partnerships (also known as corporations), along with other government partners—religious groups, educational systems, media giants, political and scientific think tanks—that, in too many cases, accumulate power and money, and further their institutional goals, by making matters of violation and peace very confusing.

The following chapters seek to clarify the waters muddied by the messages of such institutions. Why is this important? While most of us would like to see ourselves as heroes who are generally defending the innocent and promoting free and respectful interaction, we are often defending the violators and promoting violent interaction! Therefore; we must look at the most important skill that an Awakening Hero must have—the skill of *critical thinking*.

Critical Thinking

Awakening Heroes recognize that moving to a world of greater peace, freedom and justice requires critical thinking. First, let's look at the alternative—lazy dependent thinking. At the My Lai Villages, many U.S. soldiers engaged in lazy dependent thinking. They *depended* on the *thinking* of "superior" officers to choose their actions, which involved killing Vietnamese villagers, innocent or otherwise. Their thinking was *lazy* in that they did not make the effort to determine whether they were truly defending the innocent or simply violating human beings.

Here is the result of these individuals using dependent lazy thinking at My Lai: They killed numerous unarmed, non-aggressive children, women and elderly villagers! My purpose here is not to condemn those soldiers; I truly wish for them to find peace of mind and fulfillment—just as I wish the same for all people that are currently interacting peacefully and respectfully with others and the natural world. I can't state for a fact just how I would have taken action in those circumstances at 18 years of age, but we all can learn from their experiences the dangers of shutting out the primary tool of the Awakening Hero—critical thinking. In the interest of moving toward a world of greater peaceful interaction and away from a world of increasing violation, let's look at our heroic example, Hugh Thompson Jr.

Our featured Awakening Hero had received similar basic training as the men on the ground, and he had orders to pursue and shoot armed "draft-aged" individuals. He likely entered the My Lai zone with the attitude "We are the good guys; they are the bad guys", but his ability to use critical thinking opened up heroic possibilities.

Although Hugh Thompson Jr. was a member of the U.S. military, he apparently was not locked in to the attitude "my team, right or wrong", nor was he permanently on board with "we are the good guys; they (the Vietnamese villagers) are the bad guys". His attitude apparently allowed that "My team is sometimes right, sometimes wrong. I will actively support my team when they are right. I will not support them when they are clearly wrong." In the course of events, his attitude was consistent: "I choose to be one of the good guys."

We now have a complete picture of the Awakening Hero as exemplified by the actions of Hugh Thompson Jr. on that day. An Awakening Hero is consistently:

1) A Defender of the Innocent
2) A Promoter of Free and Respectful Interaction
3) A Critical Thinker in Matters of Peace and Violation

With a commitment to these three qualities, the Awakening Hero's actions become a meaningful and powerful force to move all of us toward a world of increasing peace, freedom and just interaction for ALL people—A BETTER WORLD. The following chapters will explore these qualities in greater depth.

Chapter 2

Awakening Heroes Think for Themselves

As we saw in the previous chapter, how an individual thinks can have very serious consequences. The lazy dependent thinkers contributed to more killing of innocent humans, while critical thinkers reduced the killing of innocent humans. Therefore; critical thinking is the most indispensible tool for the Awakening Hero.

If you and I are going to join the ranks of Awakening Heroes—and thus contribute to making a better world—we must not only acquire this tool, but we will have to sharpen it daily and keep it readily accessible. It is a handy tool in all situations, but, realistically, in our daily lives, we often engage in lazy dependent thinking. For example, we may *depend* on critics to help us choose an entertaining movie or select a new restaurant. However; the choices in such matters do not involve violation of another human being.

As Awakening Heroes, we must consistently bring out the preferred tool—critical thinking—in all matters of peace and violation, because each time any one of us acts on or supports a wrong call, we all move toward a world of greater violation, and that is the wrong direction.

Violation meets Critical Thinking

Although there are millions of unique variations, the logic of the Awakening Hero goes something like the following: "I seek to contribute to making the world a better world. Recognizing the unacceptable misery caused by people initiating bombings, invasions, muggings, rapes, kidnappings, as well as acts of extortion, and fraud, all of which are clearly violational, I reason that, for humans, a better world must have less such violations initiated upon other humans. Further; recognizing that slavery conditions are unacceptable, I reason that a better world must offer true freedom for each and every peaceful human to express, create, and provide for their respective needs."

Having reasoned thus far, the Awakening Hero proceeds to reckon with the tools that are used by sophisticated violators throughout the world today.

The Violator's Tools—Confusion, Illusion and Delusion

In essence, a violator is an individual who takes action upon others' bodies, minds and rightful property and earnings without the others' consent. More to the point, a violator makes an invalid claim of *ownership rights* concerning someone else's body, mind, or external property and takes action accordingly.

You don't have to have the critical thinking skills of Columbo or Sherlock Holmes to discern the violational nature of purse-snatching, burglary, rape, car theft, vandalism and outright murder that occur daily in our communities. Defending fellow humans and yourself from such acts is certainly a worthy endeavor of the Awakening Hero. Major newspapers, TV and radio broadcasts provide ample coverage of individuals committing such violations.

This would be a much easier book to write if such crimes were the full scope of the Awakening Hero's work. There are hundreds of workshops, books, and videos with excellent instruction on defending oneself and others from such acts of violation, and an Awakening Hero will seek to improve their defense skills accordingly. However; the Awakening Heroes—those who are transforming the world into one of greater freedom, peace and justice—are aware of the much larger and exceedingly powerful violators operating throughout the entire world.

These violators use *confusion, illusion and delusion* upon billions of people in order to control their personal activities, take violent actions against them, and accumulate control of their money and property without their consent. This is occurring on such a large scale—in virtually every country in the world—that most people view it as "normal" and—and this is the real kicker—most people are resigned that this is the way it has to be!? Corporate newspapers and other major media do not tend to report these violators.

The sophisticated violator seeks to magically transform that which we all normally consider a violation into a "good and proper" action, one that most accept without question. To do this, he or she utilizes the tools of confusion, illusion, and delusion.

In common terms, we call these sophisticated violators con artists. The object of the con artist is to gain your trust that he is acting for your benefit.

He also may seek to persuade you that your cooperation will benefit other worthy people as well. Of course, his real object is to benefit himself at your expense as he wrongfully asserts claim to you and your possessions. This is the clever method of violating individuals, and, to pull it off, the con artist must appear to be a trustworthy and helpful member of society.

The Awakening Hero uses critical thinking to expose all types of con artists for the violators they truly are. As we'll see, critical thinking, as it is being utilized by increasing numbers of Awakening Heroes, is the first and most important tool for defending the innocent and promoting peaceful interaction—for moving toward a world of greater freedom, peace and justice.

Con artists always rely on *confusion*. Confusion involves a lack of clarity. Therefore; the con artist's tools for creating confusion begin to lose power as you return to a state of being able to think with clarity, or act with understanding and intelligence—the opposite of a state of confusion.

Con artists arouse people's emotions—fear, envy, lust, resentment, and greed—to generate states of confusion. Critical thinking establishes the disposition for intelligent reasoning over sheer emotional momentum. The last thing con artists want is a rational inquiry into their activities. This applies to all humans who prefer violating other humans over peaceful honest negotiation.

Let's focus on the second tool of violators—*illusion*. As with all the violators' tools, your cooperation is required to enable con artists to succeed. If your tool is lazy dependent thinking, the illusion is assured—in their favor. As an Awakening Hero, you must sort illusion from reality.

Enter here the three A's: *Appearances, Assumptions*, and *Assertions*. When examined un-critically, these comprise the basic ingredients of illusion.

Just questioning the three A's—the first step of critical thinking—can effectively break down the foundations of an illusion. How you proceed to act then depends on your assessment of the situation, and your level of dedication to *defending the innocent* and *promoting free and peaceful interaction*. We must avoid taking action and supporting others' actions, based on illusion. Questioning the three A's is the vital tool for dispelling illusion.

As For Delusion—Shame on Us

Apart from locking up all con artists, we will never be able to stop them from setting up false appearances of reality. Furthermore; we can't consistently stop them from passing off false assumptions as valid, and; we'll never stop them from making false assertions.

Let's explore what it is that con artists are up to. All con artists manipulate appearances, assumptions and assertions to create confusion and illusion. The Awakening Hero must use critical thinking—keeping emotions in check and questioning the three A's—to effectively prevent the violators' greatest tool of all—our own *delusion*. While we are powerless to stop con artists' attempts to create confusion and illusion, we as individuals hold the power to prevent our own states of delusion. The cliché "the blind leading the blind" describes the problem that arises when would-be heroes seek to defend the innocent and promote free and respectful interaction while in a state of delusion.

Reality-Based Evidence

That governmental institutions include many corrupt individuals is entirely uncontroversial. That nearly all "government" institutions today, by their very nature, violate basic human rights and, therefore, have a devastating impact on billions of hardworking peaceful humans throughout the world, is a reality that millions of Awakening Heroes are now exploring. This handbook invites you to join their ranks. Let's recap:

From the Old Way—Lazy Dependent Thinking—to the New Way of the Awakening Hero

The great majority of people today engage in lazy dependent thinking, which makes the con artists' work easy. They can appeal to people's emotions, especially fear, to "justify" actions that violate peaceful humans at home and abroad. In a state of unchecked fear, people are unlikely to question the morality of actions proposed to remedy a given situation. In a state of fear, people look to "authorities" for solutions.

If we lived in a perfect world, those "authorities" would consistently seek solutions that truly defend the basic human rights of peaceful humans and enhance free and peaceful interaction among all people. In other words, if modern governments were staffed only with Awakening Heroes, this handbook would be pointless. All members of modern governments, then, would consistently respect the basic human rights of others.

Unfortunately, as we shall see, governmental "authorities" are simply humans—and mostly un-heroic. They do, in fact, take actions that further their personal ambitions, and, when these actions violate the basic human rights of peaceful honest people, the sensible solution is for those peaceful honest people (you and me) to acquire the skills of critical thinking, and to share our discoveries with others.

As our numbers increase into the hundreds of millions, we, the Awakening Heroes, will be an ever more powerful check on the institutions that "promise" to defend our rights and "establish peace" while, in actuality, they are delivering violation. In order to secure their own interests—while, of course, defending their own basic human rights—these con artists use "government" force to violate the basic rights of the honest, hardworking people—you and me.

In the same manner that street con artists manipulate appearances, assumptions, and unfounded assertions, institutional con artists (just humans giving themselves titles of authority) have gained the confidence of billions of peaceful humans while stripping them of their most basic human rights.

It is the ultimate long con—a confidence game involving a complex theatre of stages and players. Awakening Heroes are the last line of defense as they are not vulnerable to the deceptions, and they are determined to consistently defend the innocent and promote free and respectful interaction.

Just what does it mean to defend the innocent? That is the subject of the next chapter.

Chapter 3

Consistently Defending the Innocent

How does the Awakening Hero recognize a calling to *defend the innocent*? How do we define the 'innocent' and how do we recognize an act of violation against the innocent?

We'll need to sharpen up our tool of critical thinking, because this is where it really comes in handy. Those who gain from acts of violation want others to engage in lazy dependent thinking. For example, Hitler and his fellow Nazis could never have gained the acquiescence and support of millions of hard-working and generally peaceful people within Germany (and many outside of Germany as well) had more of those people been equipped with the ability to sort *rationalizations* from *reality-based evidence,* or *valid reasons.*

In preparation, I would like to make some general comments about this chapter. The contents herein illustrate what may well be the greatest irony of human interaction: While the principles for discerning violational actions from peaceful actions are uncontroversial for nearly all humans, those very same humans generally ignore the principles when it comes to the actions of "their team". "Their team" has an ideology that dictates "correct thinking" that often runs counter to critical thinking. This "correct thinking" frequently promotes the violation of the basic human rights of "other teams". If your calling is to fight for "your team"— right or wrong—this book is not for you. You can seek to be a "hero" for "your team". Many have received medals for killing innocent people, destroying and stealing their property—all on behalf of "their team".

The Awakening Hero seeks the path leading to less violation of ALL humans, thus, moving toward a world of greater peace, creative expression and joyful interactions—for ALL of us.

In other words, you and I must decide whether to take action on behalf of a "team"—an organization, a corporation, a "government", or any collective with an ideology and agenda—or to take actions as an Awakening Hero, one who uses critical thinking to consistently defend the innocent and promote free and peaceful Interaction.

For those who choose the path of the Awakening Hero, it is time to define *Basic Human Rights*. As mentioned earlier, these basic rights are not controversial and apply to every peaceful human on Earth. These rights must be acknowledged first, for they clarify the principles for determining whether a given interaction is violational or peaceful.

Basic Human Rights

In my studies, I find that all ruling parties today (modern governments) claim to be defenders of *basic human rights*. We are generally told that defending basic human rights is the purpose of our respective "governments", whether that government purports to be a democracy, a republic, a form of communism or socialism, fascism, or a religious-based state.

Of course the catch always is that they—the humans with government titles—also define what those basic human rights are. However; the Awakening Hero questions their assertions defining basic human rights. Does "your government's" definition of basic human rights contain clear and consistent definitions, or are there absurdities, contradictions, and rationalizations that lead millions to confusion and conflict?

What if there exists a statement of basic human rights that nearly all individuals—using critical thinking, of course—agree with? For example; there is much disagreement whether institutional education at others' involuntary expense is a basic right or not. Likewise; there is similar disagreement concerning the right to institutional medical care at others' involuntary expense. At the same time, there is almost no disagreement that a human has the right to freely and respectfully obtain higher learning and health treatments—for them-selves and for those they care about.

In her conversation with Phil, Lucia presents the criteria for valid statements of basic human rights, followed by a scenario that illustrates a broad range of violations of basic human rights.

Here are the established criteria for statements of basic human rights. Valid statements of basic human rights must:

- Set the most essential parameters of acceptable human interactions
- Be universally applicable to each and every mature human
- Describe rights that are inalienable
- Describe rights that bestow obligations upon others that are possible for those others to fulfill
- Not be self-contradictory (The enforcement and defense of the stated right cannot properly violate the basic human rights of non-violating humans)

As you may recall, Lucia then presents a scenario involving a home invasion. A stranger trespasses your property, vandalizes your garden, enters your home, takes sexual liberties upon your person, ties you up and imprisons you in your closet. He finds your money, and further threatens to trespass the rooms of your family members in order to take physical actions upon them.

The exercise is entirely unpleasant for a good reason; the stranger's actions are undeniably violational. Why? That is the ultimate question of all time for all of humanity. We all know the answer.

The fenced boundary is your boundary. The garden is your garden. The house is your house. The sandwich is your sandwich. The stripped, molested, and confined body is your body. The money is your money. The children are your children.

You hold a just claim of ownership control of all those things. The stranger has no just claim of ownership control of any of those things. He would properly have to obtain your permission to take any degree of control of those things, and even then, he would properly need to comply with any conditions you set concerning his control of any of those things.

Further, were he to be in possession of an "official" ID or badge, granted to him by some "official" agency, he would still properly have to have similar permission from you. If the majority of your community voted in favor of his actions, he would still properly need to obtain your permission. If the majority of your community voted for a council or congress of people to pass a law granting him "authority" to take the indicated actions, he would still properly need to obtain your permission. You have a just claim of ownership control of those things. Clearly; life would be intolerable were this not so.

Fortunately; the vast majority of people know full well this is so. The vast majority of humans would not trespass on someone's justly-owned land, intrude into his or her home, or take food and money from that home. Nor would they take actions upon the occupants within, without their permission.

Oddly, however; most of them support "government" people taking such actions—with or without the owners' permission—but we will soon see how critical thinking can clear up that anomaly. For now, we are determining a satisfactory statement of basic human rights—one that meets our list of requirements for such a statement.

As disclosed in Lucia and Phil's discussion, there is a statement that does so quite well. Again, since children may (or may not) properly be within the control of other humans, we will confine our statement to people of a responsible age (herein referred to as adults):

Every Adult Human Being Has the Basic Human Right to Full Ownership of his or Her Body, Mind, and Justly-Acquired Properties and Earnings.

Because humans must properly be able to create and procure essential things, such as shelter, clothing, food, etc., it is important to add an additional statement that provides the freedom to respectfully do so. The statement is naturally derived from the first statement, and acts to affirm our freedom:

Every Adult Human Has the Basic Human Right to Honestly and Respectfully Interact with Other Humans and the Natural World Free of Coercion and the Threat of Coercion from other Humans

These statements are vital to the work of Awakening Heroes, so let's apply some tests to verify their applicability. Do they meet the criteria for valid statements of basic human rights? By any reasonable definition, a basic human right must:

1) Set the most essential parameters of acceptable human interactions

The absence of the two statements would clearly make life unacceptable for any rational human. Furthermore; the fulfillment of the statements facilitates secure, creative, and fulfilling interaction among humans.

2) Be universally applicable to all

The two statements apply equally to all adult humans.

3) Describe rights that are inalienable

The two statements indeed describe rights that are so fundamental to the experience of being human that you or I could not give them away and still maintain an acceptable human experience

4) Describe rights that bestow obligations upon others that are possible for those others to fulfill

It is easy for another or others to fulfill the obligations required by the two statements. They need only obtain the right-holder's consent or choose to not interact at all with the right-holder.

5) Not be self-contradictory

The fulfillment of either statement facilitates the fulfill-ment of the other statement. They clearly do not contradict each other. Fulfillment of the statements would clearly not violate any-one's rights as provided by the statements.

You must determine for yourself whether the statements meet the above criteria before continuing. Note that every single matter legitimately put before a judge concerns claims of owner-ship and alleged violations thereof.

Thousands of people spend years in law schools through-out the world and, either fail to grasp, or refuse to acknowledge, this absolutely primary understanding of just interaction among all humans. The Awakening Hero explores this to the deepest levels for him or her-self.

You must apply critical thinking to explore the signifi-cance of *True Ownership Rights* in all matters of human interac-tion. The answers cannot properly be appropriated from "experts", "authorities", and various institutional pronouncements. And, of course, you absolutely must not simply take my word on such pro-found matters. On matters such as this, you must think for your-self.

Defending the Innocent—Conclusion

In matters of human interaction, a better world is a world of less violation between humans. Not controversial. However; the next statement requires critical thinking, because it is not emphasized in "government" schools, nor is it discussed thoughtfully in major media. Basic human rights arise from each and every peaceful human's true ownership of their respective bodies, minds and justly-acquired properties and earnings. Without recognition of such ownership, no human or group of humans can ever meaningfully claim violation.

Every single court trial concerning an alleged violation of one human by another human is based on ownership rights! Who has rightful claim of ownership (of a given body, mind or property) and who asserted wrongful claim of ownership? Did the rightful owner consent to the other's use of his or her body, mind or property or did the other violate a valid claim of ownership? Can you imagine any individual you know that does not assert the right of ownership of his or her body, mind and honestly-acquired property and earnings?

You may well ask: Given this basic human right of true ownership, how can humans reasonably interact? How can one human interact with another human's body, mental activity, and/or property without violating that human? How can any of us interact, trade and commune with each other at all? The answer is well-known to all:

We must obtain another's consent.

Of course you must do so without the use of force, without threats, and without deception (remember con artists). Yes; you must peacefully and honestly negotiate with the owner. Burglars, thieves, con artists, rapists, murderers, invaders, arsonists, vandals—all such criminals do not care for the inconvenience of that requirement. A person must peacefully and honestly negotiate for the use of others' bodies, minds, property and earnings. Criminals opt for violational means to do what they want to do with others' bodies, minds, properties and earnings. Isn't that the very definition of a criminal?

The Awakening Hero, on the other hand, holds a view that is opposite to the criminal's view—that, in order to defend the innocent consistently, the Awakening Hero must respect each and every peaceful human's ownership rights—consistently. Not when it's "convenient". Not only when it's "my team". Not just when it "works out for me and mine". And not only when "my authority figure says so". Violation is Violation.

Furthermore; each and every peaceful individual—no matter the country he or she inhabits; no matter his or her vocation, income level or property holdings; no matter what sex, spiritual beliefs or color of skin—each and every peaceful human is as worthy of respect regarding their basic human rights as any and all others. Those basic human rights can only have meaning if they are derived from the right of true ownership of one's body, mind and honestly-acquired property and earnings.

1) *The Awakening Hero Defends the Innocent Consistently.*

2) *To do so, The Awakening Hero defends the Basic Human Rights of each and every peaceful (non-violating) human consistently.*

3) *Therefore; the Awakening Hero defends the ownership rights of each and every human, without which violation cannot even be determined to exist among humans.*

Before proceeding to the next chapter, I invite you to truly think for yourself—critically and independently—to evaluate the validity of such a calling. The challenge is this: It is a calling that supersedes all political ideologies and "authorities". It supersedes the dictates of all institutions, be they scientific, religious, educational, "governmental", family, corporate, economic, or otherwise; so that any institution that dismisses it must necessarily become an advocate for condoning, if not actively perpetrating, further violation among humans. Yet; every institution that I'm aware of states to its members and all who will listen, that their "team" promotes basic human rights, peace, freedom....

The Awakening Hero uses critical thinking, calling for reason—not rationalization—to distinguish peaceful acts from violational acts.

Chapter 4

The Awakening Hero Consistently Promotes
Free and Respectful Interaction

Promote: Further the progress of (something, esp. a cause, venture, or aim); support or actively encourage; give publicity to

Free [interaction]: Not under the control or in the power of another; able to act or be done as one wishes

Respectful [interaction]: To feel or show deferential regard for [another's rights]

—The Free Dictionary

Some eloquent quotes follow that portray the promotion of free and respectful interaction among humans:

"First: Let us examine our attitude toward peace itself. Too many of us think it is impossible. Too many think it unreal. But that is a dangerous, defeatist belief. It leads to the conclusion that war is inevitable—that mankind is doomed—that we are gripped by forces we cannot control.

We need not accept that view...is not peace, in the last analysis, basically a matter of human rights—the right to live our lives without fear of devastation...we shall also do our part to build a world of peace where the weak are safe and the strong are just." —John F. Kennedy, Commencement Address at American University, June 10th, 1963 (five months before he was killed).

"Those of us who love peace must organize as effectively as the war hawks. As they spread the propaganda of war, we must spread the propaganda of peace. We must combine the fervor of the civil rights movement with the peace movement. We must demonstrate, teach and preach, until the very foundations of our nation are shaken. We must work unceasingly to lift this nation that we love to a higher destiny, to a new plateau of compassion, to a more noble expression of humane-ness." —Martin Luther King, Jr., "The Casualties of the War in Vietnam", Speech delivered in Los Angeles February 25th, 1967

*"Disarm now, discard and bury divisive[ness] for the sa-
ke of peace/ Seek to resolve existing differences peacefully and
intelligently with the pen and not the sword/ Somalis, bury the
hatchet, let there be no more slaughtering, and ordain peace as a
priority issue for deliberation/ Anti-peace elements and belliger-
ent men who are yet unprepared for it/ We are ready to challenge
them and convince them to join the peace process/ Somali women,
whichever your country of abode, be reminded of action on this
obligation/ Somali womenfolk, strive to keep your war-mongering
men in the bounds of morality/ Wives should preach peace and
reconciliation to their partners at home/ Where are the writers
and university professors, and why don't they produce peace liter-
ature? Why don't you propagate and consolidate peace regardless
of your clan origin?"*—Elderwoman of Somalia Adar Abdi
Fiidow, quoted from article by Mohamed Haji Ingiriis
(www.insightonconflict.org)

I could not possibly express it better! The above messages were expressed by Awakening Heroes of entirely different
backgrounds and levels of influential power.

The dual objectives of the Awakening Hero (Consistently
Defend the Innocent/ Consistently Promote Free and Peaceful Interaction) can be seen as two sides of one coin. There is the negative peace side—defending the innocent from violators—which we
dealt with in the previous chapter.

Now, we are dealing with the positive peace side of the
coin—promoting peace. No matter which side of the coin you tend

to favor, more peace coins are put into circulation each time you act. Just as you can't separate the front from the back of a coin, you cannot ultimately separate the dual objectives of heroic action.

If you choose to focus on consistently promoting free and peaceful interaction, it can be helpful to define basic human rights in accord with your preferred focus. Thus, I repeat our second statement of basic human rights:

Every Adult Human has the Basic Human Right to Honestly and Respectfully Interact with Other Humans and the Natural World Free of Coercion or the Threat of Coercion from Others

This statement is derived from the original statement:

Every Adult Human has the Basic Human Right to Full Ownership of His or Her Body, Mind, and Justly- Acquired Properties and Earnings

And so, this second statement only serves to add clarity for those who are drawn to promote free and respectful interaction. Like the two sides of any coin, the two statements are inseparable.

For the Awakening Hero, we hereby present the complete Statements of Basic Human Rights:

1) *The Right to Full Ownership of His or Her Body, Mind and Justly-Acquired Properties and Earnings*
2) *The Right to Honestly and Respectfully Interact with Other Humans and the Natural World Free of Coercion or the Threat of Coercion from Others*

We could replace millions of complex and confusing laws with one simple law:

Respect others' basic human rights.

Well, most of us could. As a matter of fact, most of us go about our lives—socializing, trading, and generally interacting with other humans and the natural world—while simply abiding that one law! But, people identifying with "government" institutions, as they exist today, can't bring themselves to do it.

On all levels, "government" people, directly and/or indirectly, violate basic human rights. In this handbook, I don't just compare "government policy" people and their institutional partners to con-artists. I am stating that they are con-artists. Many readers see the business world—"free-market enterprise" or "capitalism", etc.—as the violators, but no private business-person can "legally" violate a person's basic human rights on his or her own.

Such business-people need to partner with "government authorities" to engage in "legally" violating others' basic human rights.

Thus; you have government charters for "privileged" businesses. Corporation status is the common avenue to obtain special privilege, special exemptions from accountability, and, in effect, a way to use government force to escape the normal and just competition of truly free-market enterprise. Remember, the major auto makers in the U.S. could not have "legally" stopped the Tucker car's production. They had to do it indirectly, utilizing federal government agencies to "legally" obstruct production of the Tucker Sedan.

The Awakening Hero seeks to promote free and peaceful interaction. This refers to social interaction, all business/trade/money interaction, and certainly all "governmental" interaction. Why would any human, interacting in any given capacity whatsoever, properly have license to violate the basic human rights of any other human or group of humans?

Is a basic human right sometimes a basic human right...then it's not...then it is? Are there magical people who have the power to turn a basic human right into a silly afterthought, simply because they determined it thusly? Isn't a basic human right a BASIC HUMAN RIGHT? Those who seek to gain by violating others will come up with rationalizations to justify their actions. We will explore four principles that act to counter specious arguments used to "justify" violating others' basic human rights.

Rationalization-Buster #1

No human can know with certainty the true motives resid-ing in another human's mind.

As a mother gathers the remains of family members blown to pieces during a bombing raid, she would likely question the stated motives for the raid—"to bring democracy and freedom to her people" (if someone were insane enough to console her with such an assertion).

Every person must also question such stated motives as well, because those who choose to violate innocent people will often state goodly motives to gain support for their horrible actions. Of course, the assertion that having one's family blown to pieces serves to "bring democracy and freedom" to those people is stomach-turning of itself. But, the point here is to maintain wariness for virtuous motives that are parroted throughout the major media—particularly in reference to horrendous violations that are being committed. Simply put, critical thinkers do not believe themselves to be mind-readers.

Nor do they believe anyone else is a mind reader while assessing violational and non-violational actions that are being proposed. You would have to be a mind reader to definitively know another's motive for choosing a given course of action.

Publicizing statements of goodly motives is a common ploy to obtain support from lazy dependent thinkers. Our additional Rationalization-Busters make motives irrelevant anyway, but, it is useful to avoid being lulled into their spell in the first place. You will be much more effective in applying your critical thinking skills if you dismiss "goodly motive" tactics altogether.

Rationalization-Buster #2

For every challenge met by a community of humans; just as there are myriad violational solutions that may be considered, there are also myriad non-violational solutions that may be considered as well

As Awakening Heroes, who seek to defend the innocent and promote peaceful interaction, we can eliminate violational actions from the list of "solutions" and still find myriad non-violational actions to choose from.

When JFK stated, "Let us examine our attitude toward Peace itself...Too many of us think it is impossible...Too many think it unreal...But that is a dangerous, defeatist belief", he was touching on this very truth. In the realm of peaceful solutions, there are potentially infinite numbers of non-violational actions to consider for any given situation.

Rationalization-Buster #3

In the realm of human interaction, no human can know with certainty what will be the long-term outcome of a proposed action—violational or non-violational—initiated upon a population of people.

To quote Lucia, "It's a bit like throwing a feather into a tornado and determining where it will end up tomorrow. There simply are too many variables. This is true in the realm of human interaction as well. I can't even determine how my mate will react to an action I take with any serious degree of accuracy, much less my entire community of unique humans—humans responding to unsurmisable sets of variables—each carrying unique past experiences, cultural backgrounds, fears, and desires.

What about an entire nation of humans? I can make an educated guess; I can speculate, postulate, but; no matter how much information I gather, I'm still venturing a guess—the product of my imagination at best. I may have PhD's, be a respected "authority", an expert. I may be looked upon as a very wise man. I'm still applying my imagination—along with my biases, wishful thinking, and knowledge deficiencies—to produce my own best guess as to the future outcome of a chosen action imposed upon the realm of human interaction."

Rationalization-Buster #4

In the realm of human interaction; while the intended outcome of a proposed action can only be the product of one's mind—and, therefore, is unreal—an action taken in the here and now—whether it be violational or non-violational—IS REAL.

To quote Lucia again, "A proposed action, once taken, exists in reality. If it is a peaceful action, then a peaceful action is really occurring in the world. No guesswork, no speculation. Peaceful interaction is happening and humanity is better off for it. If a violational action is taken, then basic human rights are being violated in the here and now reality. Greater violation is happening in the world, and humanity is worse off for it. In reality!"

For you, the reader, these are only assertions, until you have applied your tool of critical thinking to each of them, questioned them mercilessly, and determined their truthfulness for yourself.

Rationalization vs. Reason

In order to promote peaceful interaction consistently, the Awakening Hero applies the four Rationalization-Busters to challenge those who promote violational actions. These principles invalidate all assertions that "justify" violating anyone's basic human rights.

The simple truth is this: Promoters of violation offer *rationalizations* rather than *reasons*. Promoters of free and peaceful interaction reject rationalizations and demand reasons. This can effectively be achieved by applying the Rationalization-Busters. In the guise of promoting and defending basic human rights, "government" and "government"-partnered institutions are generally nothing more than groups of individual humans claiming ownership control of peaceful humans' bodies, minds, property, and earnings, without obtaining the consent of those people—the very definition of violation in the realm of human interaction.

Millions of acres of property have been confiscated from rightful owners, along with the equivalent of trillions of their dollars. Those very dollars are fraudulent currency imposed on hardworking people by force and threat of force. For billions of people, the freedom to peacefully and freely pursue their dreams and maintain the security and livelihood of their families has been impeded and/or blocked entirely. Most tragically, millions of peaceful humans have been killed or maimed by "government" people.

At My Lai, the sergeant on the ground wanted to blow up innocent children with a grenade. Hugh Thompson Jr. said, "I think I can do better than that." Similarly, the Awakening Hero today observes the institutions of "government" that violate basic human rights of billions and suggests, "I think we can do better than that!" Even more confidently: "I know I can do better than that!"

Summary

First and foremost, the Awakening Hero seeks to take actions that make the world a better world, a world of diminishing violation and increasingly free and peaceful interaction among humans. Reasoning leads the Hero to the dual mission as follows:

1) Consistently Defend the Innocent (including oneself) from violators.
2) Consistently Promote Free and Respectful Interaction.

Because there is a great deal of confusion as to what defines violational vs. peaceful interaction, the Awakening Hero must develop the skill of critical thinking. In this way, the Awakening Hero can sort the matters out for him or herself, and, if called for, provide critical reasoning to others. The primary reason for the confusion arises from violators' efforts to obscure, and/or make anonymous, their acts of violation.

Very quickly, the Awakening Hero finds a need to define once and for all what our basic human rights are. Without basic human rights, no claims of violation can be said to exist.

While most individuals accept the definitions provided by institutional "authorities" concerning basic human rights, the Awakening Hero recognizes the possibility that violators may be acting—under the "authority" of the institutions—to create confusion on such crucial matters.

Out of loving respect for him or herself, for family, friends and the greater community of humanity, the Awakening

Hero questions the appearances, assumptions and assertions put forth by institutional "authorities"—especially those concerning basic human rights and the violation or respect thereof.

Just as one finds it impossible to discern violation from respectful interaction minus basic human rights, one finds it equally impossible to define basic human rights without the concept of true ownership. If a human does not have true ownership of his or her body, mind, and justly-acquired properties and earnings, there can be no claim of violation concerning that human.

For example, unless a given woman holds a just claim of ownership of her body, mind, properties and earnings, another person can rightfully take any action he or she chooses upon that woman's body, mental activity, property, and hard-earned money, without her consent—and be in the right! That is clearly unacceptable.

Therefore; a claim of ownership of one's body, mind, respectfully-acquired property and earnings, is inseparable from one's basic human rights, such that any statements of basic human rights must properly be derived from one's claims of ownership. An ownership claim is defined by a boundary which others may respect by not trespassing.

We each of us properly act as rational governors of others as we advise our friends, family, acquaintances, and business associates how they may properly respect our boundaries. Simultaneously, we govern our own actions, so that we may act respectfully concerning others' boundaries. That is the proper description of respectful government.

We cannot reasonably expect external agents, people who are not actually involved in the complex interactions of boundaries under consideration, to effectively sort these matters out for us.

Were it so that excluding others was the only option for respecting one another's boundaries, it would be a cold world indeed. Fortunately, human interaction is enhanced by the intermingling of boundaries. To do so, we simply obtain others' consent. Free and respectful interaction is the result, along with new creative solutions, adventures, games, laughter, stories, sex, music, sharing of foods, services—the endlessly fascinating interplay of humanity.

Epilogue

I have sought to define the qualities of the Awakening Heroes who are truly contributing to the betterment of humanity. For many thousands of years, gross violations of basic human rights have been perpetrated by humans who claim authority over other humans. Such "authority" had previously been proclaimed under the guises of monarchical "legitimacy", divine ordainment, or both.

As millions of people wised up to such nonsensical claims of authority, "constitutions", which are some sort of magical documents of authority, evolved, along with their "legitimate" law-making bodies, judicial "authorities", and enforcers (police and military).

Individuals who claim such authority have partnered with institutions of business and banking, media, education, the sciences and more to maintain such delusions as:

1) You, as an individual, are powerless to defend the innocent and promote peaceful interaction without authoritative and coercive institutions.

2) There is a hopeless scarcity of food, water, money, time etc., so that coercive institutions are required to manage these resources.

3) Right and wrong are complicated matters, and YOU are not qualified to sort it out for yourself.

4) Moneys—any currencies of exchange—must be managed by coercive institutions.

5) "Democratic representation", or any form of "majority rules" is a valid affirmation of coercive authority.

6) The violation of basic human rights is generally necessary and is good and right when authorized by "government" humans (including confiscation of money and properties, the destruction of vital infrastructures, and the murder of people "over there", also known as war).

I hereby assert that you, as an Awakening Hero, are fully empowered to explore the above delusions that dis-empower billions throughout the world. It is an urgent matter.

Economies, based on counterfeit currency systems, will run their corrupt inflationary course, likely leading to widespread panic and violence. More wars will ensue. Violence in the streets will be met with further violence.

Study the basics of money, including arguments for and against government-enforced currencies. Study the deeper truths of war activities, including the unpublicized activities of violational forces referred to as the CIA, Secret Service, FSO, Mossad, MI6, etc. Question everything reported by media outlets that are associated with corporate/government interests.

For now, the only meaningful solution must involve the awakening of millions to the heroic calling to:

Defend the Innocent Consistently

Promote Free and Respectful Interaction Consistently.

Think Critically

Think For Yourself

www.ingramcontent.com/pod-product-compliance
Lightning Source LLC
Chambersburg PA
CBHW021210290526
45796CB00005B/24